The Bride

Images of the Church

Daniel Berrigan

Icons by
William Hart McNichols

ORBIS BOOKS

Maryknoll, New York 10545

The Catholic Foreign Mission Society of America (Maryknoll) recruits and trains people for over-seas missionary service. Through Orbis Books, Maryknoll aims to foster the international dialogue that is essential to mission. The books published, however, reflect the opinions of their authors and are not meant to represent the official position of the society. To obtain more information about Maryknoll or Orbis Books, please visit our website at www.maryknoll.org.

Library of Congress Cataloging-in-Publication Data

Berrigan, Daniel
    The bride : images of the church / Daniel Berrigan ; icons by William Hart McNichols.
      p. cm.
    Includes bibliographical references.
    ISBN 1-57075-305-9 (paper)
    1. Christian saints – Meditations. 2. Christian martyrs – Meditations. 3. Icons – Meditations. 4. Christian saints – Poetry. 5. Christian martyrs – Poetry. 6. Christian poetry, English. I. McNichols, William Hart. II. Title.

BX4661 .B47 2000
282'.092'2 – dc21
[B]

                                             99-055608

To
Marjory Hart McNichols
and
Frida Berrigan

Contents

Foreword

Icons

The Eye of God in the Eye of the Beholder

Megan McKenna

The icon is God in a human house. It can be seen as an enclosure of divinity in a small window or a door that humbly invites those who bend before it in body or spirit into the realm of faith. Icons are celebrations, proclamations of the mystery of the Incarnation: flesh and bone rendered in gesso and gold paint painstakingly, truthfully expressed both in the finished form and in the process of the making. The making is a deliberate work, an intense labor of emptying out, of absorbing the Holy and letting remnants remain behind on board and wood. The iconographer strains muscles, bending to draw near the features he seeks to portray, momentarily making visible what is invisible to the human eye. The iconographer sits, sees, stares, and tries not to blink as truth, a speck of truth, is made manifest, made clear to those who stop and gaze upon it.

The icon declares: Halt! And what brings us to a halt makes us cease emotion. All emotions are portrayed, yet all somehow are brought to a full stop: terror, grief, utter isolation, violence, joy, rage, tenderness, even prayer itself. When emotion is held still, then prayer itself stops and is sustained or held before the mind and body. In this stasis it is sometimes called contemplation. An icon is fashioned to portray a person's meaning through God's eye — so an icon demands that we slow down, stop, be still, stand, and barely breathe. It is the presence of the Spirit coming through the eyes, and it hovers before us silently screaming: be still — you are in the presence of the Holy. You stand now on holy ground. Be attentive!

The work and vocation of an iconographer are therefore described as "wording or writing an icon." The icon is akin to the evangelist's gospel, the preacher's sermon, the teller's story. Each builds a small house for God . . . or better yet, an inn, a wayside rest, a corner of the world that becomes habitable, a sanctuary in the midst of rabble and more useful objects. Sometimes icons are done in threes — a triptych — three to a house where friends who were together in the realm of the Holy can now visit others who seek after the Holy hidden right before our eyes in the world at large. We can linger in their company, their presence, for awhile. They give the same sense of what is known when a locket is opened and a loved one is caught sight of or when a place is designated a refuge, a state of mind and soul that speaks of God-in-flesh, an image where humankind can be embraced by God and bend back toward that presence that holds us near and dear always.

At the same time an icon is confinement, like a seed in the ground, a child forming and expanding in the womb, and it is meant to give birth to Another in our midst, in our souls. Icons are mirrors, often small enough to be hand-held, that pull us close, not only to our own faces but toward the faces of those who now see face-to-face with God, as we all mightily hope to do ourselves one day. These countenances can appear intimidating, fascinating, off-putting, freeing, frustrating, purifying, indwelling, even drawing us to gasp for air or incline in worship. But there is no way to ignore them. Their presence is far too strong.

This has been the case since the fourth century, when icons were first conceived. They provoked such disturbances in people's souls and faith that their history begins in a violent controversy rooted in the nature of how theology is done and expressed, how God-talk is rendered in human expressions. The larger issue of revelation and what is deemed acceptable in describing or attempting to evoke an experience of God is found in these images. The mystery of the Incarnation, of God made human, of God in our flesh and blood and bone who came to us in history and who dwells with us until forever, is caught for an instant in these pictures and figures that exude spirit and energy that can accost us in our belief. The controversy still rages today, though expressed in different theologies and spiritualities. Can the person of God and those we reverence as holy — saints, angels, the Mother of God, martyrs, prophets, even the Trinity — be made by human hands for veneration by others? Can these images lead us to the presence of God, or do these images blaspheme and dishonor those they seek to portray?

In the eighth century, the Byzantine emperor Leo warred with theologians over this very question. When the dialogue broke down, he unilaterally declared that all "holy" images were inherently unholy and must be destroyed. And those who continued to make these unholy images were to be persecuted, even executed, because of their danger to true believers. For over a century and a half Christendom was torn asunder, with the ruling group inflicting terrible retribution on the dissenting group. The iconoclasts were those who disavowed all images, and the iconodules claimed the need of human beings to make images of those they worshiped and honored. Perhaps the most famous and one of the most vicious of the clashes was between Emperor Leo and John of Damascus, later to be St. John Damascene of Syria. St. John was both a crafter of words (a theologian) and a writer of icons (an iconodule), and he adamantly refused to obey the edict of the emperor. His defense was the body of Jesus, the mystery of the Incarnation which unequivocally proclaimed the goodness of human flesh and God's own appropriation of the human image to reveal himself to the world. And if prophets and kings had longed to see him, then all humankind could be privileged to see him depicted in human form.

When the emperor could not stop St. John's words or his writing of icons, he resorted to treachery. He sent a letter to the Syrian caliph and enclosed a letter forged in John's handwriting that convicted John of treason against the caliph. The emperor suggested that the caliph deal with John as he saw fit. John was summoned and confronted with the letter. In the next moment he was punished: by having the offending hand severed with a scimitar, the hand to be chewed upon by the dogs of the court. Poor John grabbed his hand back, clasping it tightly to his wrist and calling upon the Mother of God in his pain, crying out for vindication and help. Immediately his hand was made whole, with the public testimony of the Mother of God, who obviously approved of John's icon-painting!

Soon after, John wrote an icon in thanksgiving for the Mother of God's intervention and her kindness to him. She is depicted carrying the Child but with a third hand in the center of the icon. Her own hands hold her Son, and her third hand extends to those who cry out to her. Over the centuries that third hand has also come to stand for our own hand extended to those in need — her hand in the world now. But this history and hagiography remind us forcefully of the anger and violence that the making of holy images can stir up in Christians.

The reverence given to these images, these windows into another level of where the Spirit dwells, has been ritual since their genesis. They are attended by candle flame, lamp oil, smoke, and incense. When an image is finished, it is not done. In fact it is just beginning its work, its wording. It is just beginning to be a sustaining presence. When placed in a room, it solidly takes over the space, eventually drawing all the space toward it in a pinpoint, a target, a home base. The icon holds the place together and draws all to itself because at its heart it is a threshold, beckoning us to risk entering, to be still, to listen, and to know that we are always in the presence of God, but especially so here in this place. In those moments the icon is also shelter for awhile, from the storms and demands of earth. It invites. Come. Rest. Know and be known. Be still and empty, emptied out. Make a room for God — the size of an icon — in your soul. Because of this invitation and power, this presence that beckons, one can feel affection for icons, like one does for old and dear friends and loves.

Who are these people depicted in icons — faces, eyes wide-set, long noses, high brows, hands positioned ritually, looking at another, pointing, looking straight out at us? Who are they who question, challenge, comfort, and demand that we become conscious of ourselves and of God, and in so doing become true, become human, become holy, become those who belong to God? They are our forebears, ancestors in the faith, patriarchs and matriarchs of old, prophets and dreamers, models, old friends, believers who struggled and made it home free, companions on our way, guardian spirits concerned with our safety, our bodies' and souls' well-being, our communities and churches.

They are fellow-travelers, strangers, anonymous or even unknown saints who sinned and repented, agonized over evil, and repaired their portion of the world. Mary Oliver, a contemporary poet and winner of the Pulitzer Prize and National Book Award, in her book *Winter Hours: Prose, Prose Poems, and Poems* writes of her own mentors, teachers, and luminaries. She is describing writers and poets, the voices she hears when she writes, but she could be describing the faces and persons depicted in icons for us as well:

> ... spirits whose influence and teachings I am now inseparable from and forever grateful for. I go nowhere, I arrive nowhere without them. With them I live my life, with them I enter the event, I mold the meditation, I keep if I can some essence of the hour, even as it slips away. And I do not accomplish this alert and loving confrontation by myself and alone, but through terrifying and continual effort, and with this innumerable, fortifying company, bright as stars in the heaven of my mind.[1]

The icon, as with any symbol that is holy — a sacramental — is seen through with belief. It is bound intimately, inexorably, with tradition, history, even dogma and devotional practice. It lives in the church, in the believing community, the way a novena or benediction or the touching of the beads of a rosary lives — in the hands and minds and hearts of believers, practitioners of faith. It leads them home, inside out — to an awareness of the Holy that has always been there/here but perhaps was overlooked, missed until this moment, this time of need and power that the icon illumines and reveals.

These faces of the friends of God question us: and question us in such a way that what is posed, proposed to us, is at root unanswerable. Do you know who you are? Do you know who you belong to? Do you know what you were made for? Do you know how to live, to suffer, to die? Do you want communion, holiness, and ultimate freedom from death? You see — all these images sound us out silently. They are truth-tellers, revelations and confessors intent on laying bare our raw and well-concealed places of spirit and soul that hide and refuse to grow gracefully. And, of course, these faces comfort us, hold us in our pain and regard us and surround us with tenderness, drawing us gently and firmly into the company of those who suffer and who reach in their desperation, isolation, and agony for God's succor and strength. They, with God, seek to redeem all humankind and creation. They are about the work of transforming even terror and of wresting hope from inhumanity.

---

1. Mary Oliver, *Winter Hours: Prose, Prose Poems, and Poems* (New York: Houghton Mifflin, 1999), 20.

To look upon an icon, to gaze, to search its detail, to sit before it, to contemplate and enter its eyes, is to acknowledge, often in spite of our rational analysis, another domain, another realm altogether than the one that is visible. Like the mystery of the Incarnation — God's grasping of our flesh as presence — an icon is a covenant, a bond, a pact between God, who is limitless, and all who are created and limited, between what is unmade and what is becoming reality and truthfulness by grace's intent within us through our maker. We, in turn, are seen into and through. We are accosted, and we are invited to renew our vows, to declare our intents, and once again to kneel and to bend and to obey the demands of our God who thrives in our flesh and loves our form even unto appropriation, crucifixion, transfiguration, and resurrection. This covenant bond, this vow between God and us that is the purpose of the icon, can be described in words borrowed from Galway Kinnell's poem "The Vow":

> When the lover
> goes, the vow though
> broken, remains, that
> trace of eternity love
> brings down among us
> stays, to give
> dignity to the suffering
> and to intensify it.[2]

That is why in ritual response to this Presence, it is natural to approach the icon, bend, cross oneself three times, and kiss the image — in gratitude, in need, and in affection. Wood once again becomes a bridge that can cross the distance and let us, however fleetingly, touch the Holy. Or as the Native Peoples say — the wind on our fingertips is the Great Spirit kissing us; the wind in our hair is the Great Spirit caressing us and laying a blessing upon our heads. One must, of necessity, respond to an icon: obey its summons, if only by avoiding the niche or corner where it resides or by turning away in frustration, disgust, or ignorance. As the Celts once carved in their doorways: Bidden or unbidden, God enters in. It is so with icons as well.

---

2. Galway Kinnell, "The Vow," in *When One Has Lived a Long Time Alone* (New York: Alfred A. Knopf, 1992).

The iconographer, the painter, begins often in response to a summons — or ordinary request or commission — from a person, a group, or a church community. But this summons is always really the beckoning of the Spirit, and so the painter begins ritually with prayer and fasting. Often the image is painted by night, when it is easier to be immersed solely in the symbols, colors, gold, and gesso. Even when the iconographer sleeps or does mundane chores, the icon teaches and seeks to be expressed through the artist-laborer. Always the iconographer is there — before the icon as before power and authority. Mind and muscles quiver and strain to obey: to let the form come through fingers, as notes pour through a flute or trumpet. When it is finished and blessed and enthroned, then it begins its life of summoning forth, in earnest, in time and place. It summons all who approach it as a small incarnation of the divine seeking to seize flesh once again as a lover holds the beloved fast, or a parent holds a child secure, or a friend holds the other lightly and freely. Unspoken, unheard except in the recesses of the heart, are the words: Come! Come closer! You are on holy ground. God is here. Come closer still. Come kiss and be kissed back. Come. Obey and surrender to the Ultimate, the Transcendent, the Incarnated. Be — come.

There is an ancient Jewish story called "The Fragrance of Paradise" from the tradition of the prophet Elijah. Elijah approaches a simple rabbi who loves the Torah and studies it for long periods of time, trying to understand it, but more to love it and integrate it into his person and life. Elijah asks him: "Would you like to visit paradise for just one day?" "Of course!" is the answer. "And, Elijah," the rabbi asks, "is it true that on the Sabbath in paradise all the great ones of our tradition — Abraham, King David, Isaiah, all the prophets and saints — gather together and study Torah?" "Yes," replies Elijah. The rabbi then says, "Do you think that perhaps my one day in paradise could be a Sabbath and that I might join them in their study?"

And in a twinkling, the rabbi finds himself in paradise. It is unbelievable. He spends the whole day studying and discussing portions of the Torah, interspersed with readings and chanting of the psalms and prayers. It is a remarkable day. But to be honest the rabbi is not paying all that much attention to the conversation and discussion, because paradise smells heavenly! It is a richly fragrant presence. The very ground itself smells as it often does on earth after rain with the smells ready to jump out and seize hold of you. The flowers are strong, singular, and sweet. The air is so fresh. Even the weeds and bushes have their own distinct scent, and the trees carry familiar and strange aromas that seem stronger and more durable than on earth. He keeps breathing in deeply and thinks: if only I could take some of the fragrance of paradise back with me. Its smell would be a comfort in hard times, strength in time of doubt, and a sign that truly I had visited paradise.

Elijah arrives at the end of the day to return him to earth, and he earnestly pleads: "Would it be possible for me to take home a portion, a part of the fragrance of paradise?" Once again, Elijah's explanation and words startle him: "Yes, you may take as much as you like. Just remember that what you take to earth now will be taken from your final portion when you come to settle and stay in paradise." At once the rabbi is sure. He does not want to lose even a small portion of the life to come because of his want of it here on earth now, so he sighs and tells Elijah that he'd best go home empty-handed.

And in another twinkling he is back on earth in his house. As he wanders through the familiar rooms that somehow seem strange to him now he keeps sniffing and smelling, breathing deep and deeper still. The scent, that fragrance, is here, with him — and yet he did not bring any of it back from paradise. Where could it be coming from? Finally, he recognizes where it is lodged: on the sleeve of his garment, his robe. The robe he'd worn had dragged in the dirt, brushed over the flowers and plants, gotten snagged and caught on the trees, and been in the atmosphere the whole day. The fragrance lingered in his robe!

Immediately he removes it, and he never wears it again. He wraps his Torah scrolls in it, and early every morning he comes and breathes deeply of the fragrance of paradise. It is a good way to start out each day. And he invites all his friends, kin, and neighbors in to smell and breathe deeply of the robe's fragrance when they are tired, doubting, struggling with life, and discouraged. It always helps — this deep gulp and fragrance of paradise. God, blessed be His Name, in his great mercy had given the gift so unexpectedly and freely.

It is like that with an icon — once finished and blessed it resides on earth, but it too knows that fragrance that it carries within itself, for it was conceived there in paradise, executed with the help of the Creator and the hand of the iconographer. The scent remains and is at home with the smell of beeswax candles and smoking incense rising — these clouds reminding us of Yahweh of old's presence with his people.

From the beginning our God has been about the work of saving us, of asking us "Where are you?" (God's first words to Adam and Eve when they are outside the garden). God has been about the work of trying to draw us closer once again to himself and to assure us of his presence and intimacy in spite of not knowing our sin and reluctance to be touched and held by the Holy Unutterable One. In this presence no words are needed anymore. The icon has been written to say it all: mercy. Mercy. Mercy singing in the night, seeping through our minds and flesh and lingering like a fragrant smell in the world at large.

The icon is God's silent, boundless mercy. The icon is God's poem and song without words. The icon is God's touch, a kiss, and then the empty place that calls forever after to us — the icon is the echo of God's incarnation once and for all time upon the earth. The icon is a rest stop on the way home, a small sanctuary, a protection, a moveable feast that makes us tremble. Blessed be the Name and Form of the Holy One. Blessed be all that God has made. Glory, glory, glory in it. Amen.

Robert Frost once said: "We begin in infancy by establishing correspondence of eyes with eyes."[3] And the icon remains among us reestablishing contact and correspondence between our eyes and God's eyes. There is silence. There is presence. There is grace abounding. The Jesuit poet Gerard Manley Hopkins wrote:

I walk, I lift up, I lift up my heart, eyes,
> Down all that glory in the heavens to glean our Saviour;
> > And, eyes, heart, what looks, what lips yet gave you a
Rapturous love's greeting of realer, of rounder replies? . . .

These things, these things were here and but the beholder
> Wanting; which two when they once meet,
The heart rears wings bold and bolder
> And hurls for him, O half hurls earth for him off under
> > his feet.[4]

---

3. Robert Frost, *Collected Poems, Prose and Plays* (New York: Library of America, 1995), 742.
4. Gerard Manley Hopkins, "Hurrahing in Harvest," in *Poems of Gerard Manley Hopkins*, ed. W. H. Gardner and N. H. MacKenzie, 4th ed. (New York: Oxford University Press, 1967).

And in this place dedicated by attention to the presence, our God has the last word: Fear not. You are mine and I am yours. All yours. Come. Behold. Be Held. Come. See yourself in the Eye of the Beholder, the Eye of the Holy One. Come and stay with God awhile. This is an icon.

This collection of icons is titled *The Bride: Images of the Church*, with text by Daniel Berrigan, S.J. The ancient image of the bride spans the symbolic history of the Ancient Testament and the New Testament. It is first of all relational and eventually incarnational. The prophets, especially Hosea, revealed God and Israel in the vocabulary and relation of husband and wife, God always faithful and Israel more often than not, as with us, unfaithful. Faithfulness, intimacy, steadfastness, truthfulness, and ever-deepening commitment and love expressed and received — these give birth to the children of God and are God's hallmarks. In the person and flesh of Jesus Christ, this relationship of God with his church revealed divinity with humanness, justice with mercy, commitment with freedom, and a relationship that could be further revealed in singular and individual human beings.

This book contains many faces of Christ himself, faces that peer out at us seeking to express characteristics of Christ in history, in the church, in old and contemporary saints, and in nontraditional holy people. Each person written here in icon and print is an icon of divine love, a particular path of discipleship, a glimpse of the face of Christ written in human flesh, among us still. Women, children, men, companions, and friends of humanity — within and on the fringes of the church, some even standing in loving opposition to it and some far from its domains in this world — all say something essential and necessary for our understanding of the presence of Christ still in our midst. Each face is so personal, conceived in time and place, reminding all of us of the diversity of how God speaks to us and seeks our faces, hoping for our intimacy and proclamation to the world that the good news is God-with-us always.

This bride is blushing with new love, reaching out with arms wide flung, but she also walks alone, burdened and isolated from others because of her standing first of all next to Truth itself. She is martyr, prisoner of conscience, theologian, mystic, lonely and vigilant, a member of a community, solitary witness, husband, single woman — the litany is as endless and diverse as the faces of Christ in his church still today, in our rich and varied scripture traditions, and in believers' piety and devotion. Some of these faces are extraordinary and well-known; others are seemingly ordinary, anonymous, or known only to a few. Each is a face of Christ, revealing the Word of God among us. Each exposes a facet, like a diamond, of the church's members, all one with the Body of Christ. This body, like each face in this book, suffers, dreams, hopes, prays, struggles to believe, and stands there, stands true and kneels, forgiving, praying. And this body and these faces say with their choices and lives: we are one; we are Christ; we are the face of God walking in the world throughout history. Each one looks out at us, questioning, shimmering with expectation, waiting for our response, wounded by the world and yet shining like the "silent sea of glass" reflecting back to us that "on earth as in heaven, we are one."[5]

---

5. William Hart McNichols, S.J., "The Fourth Time I Saw the Bride," unpublished poem (November 1998).

1

Nuestra Señora de las Sandias

The Sandia Mountains, near Albuquerque, New Mexico, have always been for me one of the most hypnotic and holy places on earth. Infinite love and a sense of the Sandias as sacred mountains were poured into this icon.

A professor of Spanish at the University of New Mexico explained to me that sandia is actually an archaic Spanish word for "fiery at night." This icon is an attempt to capture the Sandias in sunset with the Mother of God and the Christ Immanuel taken from the Greek "Kykko" icon reinterpreted by the seventeenth-century Russian master Simon Ushakov. —WHM

Our Lady of the Sandias

Among those mountains
sunset or dawn
    like the measureless longing
of ungovernable hearts
    breathing, sighing —
"O would that trivial life were redeemed by
mysterium tremendum, Incarnation!"

Tremendum
that God be
ignorant from birth?
Brawn, youth,
clumsy at start?

Tremendum
infused with trivia —

Nuestra Señora de las Sandias

a mewling infant
free from his mother's arms
essays a first step, grows confident,
mimes, molds sounds
tantamount to words.

An unsubmissive gaze at length
measures the world he made.

O He shall labor upon those steeps
beyond!

      She too
the holy two —
measuring the heights in tears and blood
the coloration
of skies that shortly
make night of all, consummated.

2

Mother of God of Magadan

Magadan is a city in eastern Siberia built by Stalin to be the administrative center of the entire slave labor system for the former Soviet Union. The icon of the Mother of God of Magadan was commissioned to honor the millions of martyrs and holy ones of the Catholic and Orthodox traditions who died in the gulags, especially the three hundred Russian Orthodox bishops who gave their lives rather than submit to militaristic, atheistic communism.

Pope John Paul II has said that the true perestroika is a reunion of the Christian traditions of the East and of the West: the Holy Orthodox Church and the Roman Catholic Church. —WHM

~

The Mother

"Behold
the tree, deterring—

"on flesh
incised—
a warning

"havoc
if you will
our holy place,
distain the coin,
heal, reconcile—
all at risk—

"no one so high
but
one brute blow
brings low."

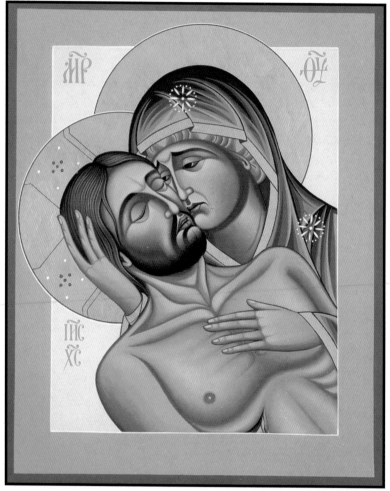

Mother of God of Magadan

Nonetheless
Mary mother,
    stands.

How praise you?
I shall not praise.
    Another praises you ...

3

St. Joseph, Shadow of the Father

*St. Joseph is patron of Canada; of other countries; of numerous con-
gregations of women and men; of contemplatives, fathers, husbands,
carpenters, and all workers; and of the hope for a "happy" death, because of his being assisted by the Mother of God and Jesus Christ
at the time of his own death, which is commemorated on March 19.
Pope John XXIII named St. Joseph patron of the universal church and
gave him a second feast day on May 1, the feast of St. Joseph the
Worker.*

*The title of this icon was inspired by the profound and beautiful
book with this name by Father André Doze of Lourdes. The red clothing on St. Joseph and the Holy Child come from a description of a
"vision of Peace" seen by the children of Fátima on October 13, 1917.*

— WHM

Joseph, Plowman, Speaks

She crossed a field
bearing the Child
into a shadowy grove,
then
sat to weaving,
head bowed, fingers flying —
a busy stillness at the heart.

And about her and the Child,
and the tree
(still, still as Mary),
circle upon circle
I wove a furrow —

St. Joseph, Shadow of the Father

like earning and entering
paradise;
labor, then mild joy.

At the still center, she
and the Child aimlessly gathering
wild grasses in hand —
the scattered leaves
gathering
of the universe.

Tools (Joseph Speaks)

To be a part of things, to be apart from them.

I watched from a doorway, artisans
summon out of a dumb stick some form of beauty,
the grain emerging along hand or arm like a pulse,
every sigh of the blade saying, I did not do this.

Or parlayed with old trees in my yard
that shift painfully in the wind, heads together
nodding memory awake.
        I did not lead them there.
They were already old when my father slept
a drowsy noon in their shade.

I had even less to do with the stars
that led me to her, that bring her still face to me
evening and dawn, making of evening and dawn
one tranquil ecstasy.

4

Nuestro Salvador de las Sandias

I was so inspired by the beautiful snow scenes in Dreams, *a film by the Japanese master Akira Kurosawa, that when I began this icon of the Risen Savior I was still seeing the world in snow. A landscape of fallen snow seemed also an appropriate symbol for the silence of death and the tomb of Christ.*

Our Savior of the Sandias, set against the shrouded, holy Sandia Mountains, bears a budding cottonwood branch, one of the earliest signs of spring in New Mexico. He blesses us with his wounded hand and the peace of the postresurrection apparitions recorded in the gospel of John. —WHM

Savior of the Sandias

"He took with him Peter, James, and John, and went up onto a mountain to pray. While he was praying his face changed in appearance and his clothing became dazzlingly white. . . . Peter and those with him had fallen into a deep sleep; but awakening, they saw his glory."
(Luke 9:28–29, 32)

Peaks I dwell upon,
peak of the human, peak
of ecstasy hard earned.

Lowly too; learn of Me —
the one, the other
mountain, valley
     incompatible?
No: in comity dwelling;

the tension, the thin air
of height, of greatness credited;

Nuestro Salvador de las Sandias

below, the stifling air —
servitude.

I am campesino, born
in a cattle lean-to, less claiming
than fox or bird of dwelling place,
wandering hither & yon —

you would not for a moment grant it;
this anonymous One is
            God.
        Until, until
I breathe upon, and weave in air
like the want of wonder-working Moses
close, face to your face
this sprig of April, plucked from the Sandia.
Faith
        springs
                seasonal.
            Believe, and live.

5

Jesus Christ

Redeemer Holy Silence (Hagia Hesychia)

This rendition of an eighteenth-century Russian icon calling us into silence is naturally difficult to put into words. The enigmatic aura of this icon, which grows with silent conversation, greatly contributes to its drawing power. Holy Silence is an allegorical representation both of Christ as the feminine Sophia and of the Silence of the Suffering Servant of Isaiah's prophecy, and it is also a vision or reminder of the mystical Russian Jesus prayer. The earliest known image of Holy Wisdom as feminine comes from a manuscript of the fourteenth century from Mt. Sinai. — WHM

∾

"When he was accused by the chief priests and elders, he made no reply....He did not answer [Pilate] on a single count, much to the governor's surprise." (Matt. 27:12, 14)

Christ, diurnal silence of God,
silence between heartbeats,
silence of the pierced Heart,

silence. "No defense" —
allows
    Pilates and Herods,
like dogs, their day;
      their multitudinous henchmen —
      their "school of assassins,"
their marauding "death squads,"
their disappeared and tortured,
their gulags and death camps,

32.

Jesus Christ: Redeemer Holy Silence (Hagia Hesychia)

their demolition squads and preventive detention,
their just war apologists, abortionists,
their genetic thinkerers, "assisted suicide" spoliators,
their doomsday bunkers muttering, down-counting —

Creation be damned! The cry —
sweet world come to this; a vast lunar ossuary.

And who to weep?
    Unaccountable, this silent One,
Hagia Hesychia, her lips
moving like blind fingers upon Braille.
    Millennial, she mediates the Book of Job —
    jot and tittle
    the text
        sorrow has by heart.

6

Holy Prophet Elijah

The Old Testament prophet is given awesome treatment in Elijah, *a little book by Adrienne von Speyr, which helped me to find this holy man. Elijah is also revered as the "founder" of the Carmelites and is shown in this icon receiving bread from heaven.* —WHM

∼

An amazing cycle of stories has swirled about this wild prophet. Lively and menacing, albeit merciful, the tales reach out of antique Hebrew texts and enter pell-mell the Christian texts. There Elijah stands in our midst, in the many allusions (and illusions) concerning John the Baptist and Jesus himself.

Alban Goodier, writing of John the Baptist, has captured well the spirit of Elijah, the ancient forerunner. He describes the descendant and soul twin, the one who later "came fasting":

> . . . a weird, uncouth, unkempt, terrible figure, in harmony with his surroundings, of single mind, unflinching, fearing none, a respecter of no person, asking for nothing, to whom the world with its judgments was of no account whatever, though he shouted that he knew it through and through, . . . drawing others by no soft inducements, but by the harsh lash of his words, . . . distinguishing true heart-conversion from the false conversion of conformity. . . .

We can hardly credit it, the ferocious monotheistic passion that governs Elijah.

He conducts a mighty show of strength against the priests of Baal, and wins out. Then shortly, he proceeds to slaying with his own hands the entire coven of adversaries.

He is granted a theophany at Horeb; there, the stories surrounding Moses on the same mountain are at once repeated and corrected.

35

Holy Prophet Elijah

Moses had seen Yahweh in "earthquake, wind, and lightning"; Elijah is to know God in the "soft whisper of a breeze."

His survival is a marvel, an illuminated text urging, celebrating the providence of God, all mischance withstanding. In the wilderness Elijah is fed by ravens. Then he himself becomes a providential man; for an impoverished widow he multiplies food and oil, and even raises her son from the dead.

At the end he is swept into heaven, the first of humankind to depart this world in the flesh, his body intact and fiery. From the ascending chariot he tosses his mantle to disciple Elisha, together with a wonderful lagniappe, a "double portion" of his own spirit.

◆

The one who goes around, comes around. Enduring rumor makes of Elijah a sign of "return": his own, as a portent signaling the onset of the day of Yahweh.

Jesus clearly respected and loved his memory, even summoning him in the flesh. Elijah, representing prophecy, together with Moses, representing the law, attend the Savior at his transfiguration.

He never died, he never dies, it seems.

Again and again he enters scripture, a guerdon, a rich symbol of multiple occasions. At Nazareth, Jesus alludes to the episode of Elijah and the widow, to illustrate the rejection of a prophet by his own townsfolk.

What are we to make of this portent, this mortal rendered immortal, a prophet at once tender of heart and merciless, fierce yeoman of a fierce deity?

Alfred Delp, S.J., executed by the Nazis for his involvement with the resisting Kreisau Circle, writes from his prison cell. He describes the age of John the Baptist; it could as well be that of Elijah — or our own:

> Woe to any age in which the voice crying in the wilderness can no longer be heard because the noises of everyday life drown it — or it is lost in the hurry and turmoil of "progress" or simply stifled by authority, misled by fear and cowardice. Then the destructive weeds will spread so suddenly and rapidly that the word "wilderness" will recur to the mind willy-nilly. I believe we are no strangers to this discovery.

And again, Delp:

> O may the arresting voices of the wilderness ring out, warning in
> good time that ruin and devastation actually spread from within.
> May the Advent figure ... of the incorruptible herald-teacher in
> God's name, be no longer a stranger in our own wilderness. Much
> depends on such symbolic figures in our lives. For how shall we
> hear if there are none to cry out, none whose voice can rise
> above the tumult of violence and destruction, the false clamor
> that deafens us to reality?

Amen, and indeed.

◆

> Whether true God is vindicated
> by such a spectacle; thus —
> "Cut the bull into pieces.... Call upon your gods
> and I will call on the Lord.
>   The god who answers with fire,
> is God."
>   Then God sent fire.
>
>   And the victim consumed, Elijah:
> "Seize the four hundred fifty prophets of Baal.
> Let none of them escape."
>   They were seized,
> and Elijah slit their throats.

> Godly activity?

> And a further question:
>   What sort of God stands revealed
>   in such an episode?
>   What God
> is sought and come upon by the people?
> The question is hardly irrelevant to later times —
>   and their Baals or God.

7

St. John, Evangelist

St. John is normally portrayed in two different ways in icons: as the youthful apostle or as the aged divine or theologian. This image of the Beloved Disciple is taken from the right arm of a painted crucifix by Cimabue. John's gaze of wounded desolation at the death of the Lord begs us to have compassion. —WHM

∽

A narrator
sober, clear of eye, labors
toward birth of truth.

And lo! Another generation
learns, mourns
perfidy, dishonor,
so
exorcising their leaching power.

Learns as well —
memorizing, pacing
the heart's native ground —
nobility, high honor, self-donation.

We call him "inspired,"
a lofty sentiment
brought rude to earth —
truth, immediacy,
conturbation of spirit.

So we learn at length
act, consequence,
vainglory's chariots,

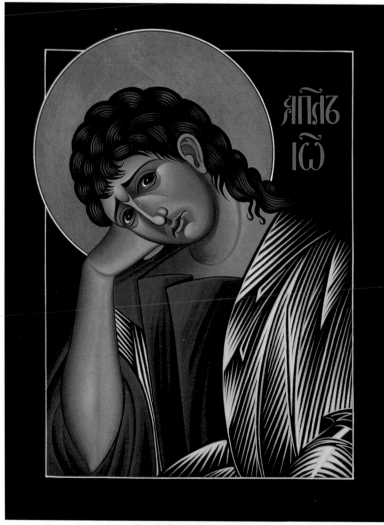

St. John, Evangelist

victory's victims —
bones dry bones.

And at center eye
One
possesses His soul,
dies then,
the tomb sealed, outlawed
against lawless mischance —
then
the violation
we name resurrection.

Say it plain.
       It is faith violated.
Say it.

Credo quia impossibile.

Faith rolls the stone aside,
timorous enters the tomb

resonant with the (sworn) word —
what could not be
and is.

8

Francis 'neath the Bitter Tree
1182–1226

This icon of the "Alter Christus," Francis of Assisi with his suffering Lord, is based on the beloved painting by the Spanish master Murillo. It was commissioned by a doctor working with people with AIDS.

—WHM

⁓

Look how his lips, eager as tongues
of fire, lap the living blood,
how close embrace
(somehow,
the arm of Christ
passionate, loosed from spread-eagling)
puts sensibilities to scandal!

Torment, toil, and trouble!
The lacerated body
leans close as a lover's
full weight upon the beloved breast.

And the sign above
bold as a billboard,
a cuneiform of guilt,
telltale with shame, dishonor
dismay, dereliction of right order,
nature's violation, religion's
strait taboo transgressed —
spells out crime and outcome.

Francis 'neath the Bitter Tree

Wash hands of Him!
  No king
but Caesar!
  Release unto us
one named Barabbas!

Francis, kiss
for our sake, the Leper.

9

The Servant of God
Mechthild of Magdeburg
1210–1297

After reading Carol Lee Flinders's portrait of Mechthild in Enduring Grace: Living Portraits of Seven Women Mystics, *I wanted to give visual expression to Mechthild's awful struggle and her bathing in "the flowing light of the Godhead" (the title of her mystical work).*

—WHM

❧

She is one of those spirits who appear now and again in the churches, sprung from God knows where, carrying through life a groaning burden of ... what? Reality?

Like Ezekiel the forbidden, she dared again and again to attempt to name the Ineffable. This was risky business. Her Lover was not in great demand in our world, nor (in any century) accorded large welcome.

A pattern emerges: rejection and scorn. Like Jesus, like daughter. Mystics are those who pay attention. The Object of their attention is supersensible, "risen" we say, for want of a better word. So the attentive ones seem to dwell in and out of this world, not greatly devoted to matters that preoccupy most of us. These "dreamers" are an annoyance, a friction to the "realists" firmly planted in the here and now.

The Mechthilds are also great critics of worldly matters; they land especially hard on a worldly church.

In pursuit of this task they are slow learners, if even that. (One is tempted to go further and say, they never learn.) They never learn (or so seldom and late as to make little difference) that a worldly

45

The Servant of God Mechthild of Magdeburg

church, when assailed, will recoil and seek revenge — in this much resembling its counterpart, the world. The urge to survive is strong; at times it grows savage. Church and state, once assailed, adopt a common method of disposing of domestic troublemakers.

No doubt Mechthild uttered her critique, knowing the danger. Beyond doubt as well she was particularly vulnerable, being a woman, and a Beguine, which is to say, not a nun, with no status to speak of.

Her anger at the worldly church issued in a blistering prose that verged on lyrical poetry. The style was the woman; and the woman fused tenderness, savagery, and skill — all the more dangerous to the status quo.

For sheer effrontery, consider this:

Alas, crown of holy church, how tarnished you have become....
Alas, crown of holy priesthood, you have disappeared,... nothing
left but... priestly power — with this you do battle against God
and His chosen friends.

This Beguine had exceeded all limit. She was ordered evicted from her refuge. Eventually, aged and blind, she was received in the Cistercian convent of Helfta. There she lived out her last years, tenderly cared for by women.

◆

Her veil and robe are palest lavender,
        a hint of green;
she is clothed, laved, swathed in contemplation,
        colors muted
            mortal life foresworn
tongue framing a faint hint of alleluia
        uttered elsewhere.

The face — wrapt, intent, inward;
        that, and one hand;
the hand too is wrapt, intent, inward,
        the instrument
of soul and its drama,
        as though it traced

in midair, the lineaments of ecstasy,
    a Form beyond form.

    And the left hand? Where
is the left hand?
    It is left to us.
Soul's quest is incomplete.

Mechthild ventures, adventures
    beyond the icon, one with the icon
as left hand is one with right —
and yet, reach exceeds grasp.
May we too hope?
    Mechthild
touches, draws close, is drawn close —
    the Face, the Embrace.

10

St. Joan of Arc with St. Michael the Archangel
1412–1431

The wonder of St. Joan of Arc is her hold on people and her steady spiritual work as a holy muse, igniting the imaginations of such disparate artists as Boutet de Monville, Mark Twain, Vita Sackville-West, Carl Dryer, Arthur Honeggar, Jean Anouilh, and Leonard Cohen.

— WHM

The brothers and their mother encouraged one another to die bravely, saying such words as these: "God is looking on, and he truly has compassion on us, as Moses declared in his canticle, when he protested openly with the words, 'And God will have pity on his servants.'"

(2 Macc. 7:5–6)

And pity on Joan likewise, this martyr who so strongly recalls the Maccabean seven and their mother.

As her "case history" shows, the wonder is not that the church at times can be unutterably corrupt, guilty of murder of the innocent, but that the church can come to a better mind, repent, and rehabilitate its victims.

Cold comfort, but better than none.

She was nineteen when she perished; the number sticks in the mind, a horror.

To execute a woman, a mere child, and this by order of bishops and canon lawyers! (Even in America, besotted as we are with death rows and daily executions, the fate of a woman on death row gives pause to the most hardened law-and-order advocates.)

49

St. Joan of Arc with St. Michael the Archangel

The furore surrounding the fate of Joan never subsided. In the minds of generations her steadfast resolve, the purity of her soul, won the day.

She could have saved herself, but she refused to recant. Let her judges be warned: she was of God. St. Michael and Sts. Catherine and Margaret had truly spoken to her.

They put her to the torch and threw her ashes in the Seine.

But it was as though the flames that consumed her burned on and on, an inflammation in the soul of the church. Four hundred and fifty years elapsed between her death and the declaration of her sanctity. Granted that the church functions as though time were of little import, as though even on earth believers stand *sub specie aeternitatis* — still, was ever repentance and vindication so delayed?

◆

Tender, awful —
    the art of a terrible equilibrium —
      flames below; above
Archangel Michael, marmoreal, untouched,
    hands supporting the manacled hands of Joan.

In the hour of great Testing,
    the Maid has prevailed, a Daniel
    in a cave of ecclesial carnivores.

    Now she is stripped like a David
of impeding armor;

      she wears
formless over her slight form,
    a shroud.

Hair wild in the firestorm, eyes
    tormented; hands to face, as though
distraught, unable to credit this caustic outcome
    of a fair dream.

    "My voices"
stilled, uncounseling.

And yet, and yet
    the great angel upbearing.

11

St. Ignatius's Vision
at the Chapel of La Storta

November 1537

St. Ignatius's Vision at the Chapel of La Storta

"*Between the lake of Bracciano and the Ponte Molle, about two hours journey from Rome, is a town called La Storta. A short distance from the road stands a half-ruined chapel. Here, in November 1537,*

St. Ignatius and his companions stopped to rest. Ignatius went in to pray. Rome lay before him, visible in the distance. He felt drawn to commend the future to the Father; and here the Blessed Trinity granted him a grace we know as the Vision of La Storta.

"Ignatius asked Our Lady to commend to her Son the designs God had inspired in him. For years he had sought to be associated with Christ, to be 'enrolled under His banner,' he and the companions God had given him.

"Ignatius fell into a rapture. He saw before him the Father, and the crucified Jesus. The father said to His son, 'Take this man as your servant.' And an immense certitude overcame Ignatius; he and his companions were to be associated for all time with Christ bearing His cross."
                                                           — Hugo Rahner, S.J.

∼

La Storta: Ignatius Speaks

It starts here.
    Nada, the all.
Everything of base use removed, vanished —
"riches, honors, credit of a great name,"
all gone, as though in whirlwind, as though
my life a genesis, a world newly accoutered.

The All.
See at center eye, a trinity of hands
divine, so human, in close conjunction,
as though planets in pure space, traced
paths unheard of prior.

    And above, looming
dark, threat and weight,
the cross, a procrustean bed
bends Christ double
to living cruciform.

O they shall stretch upon it,
for trial of stature

and raise upon the world
for countersign, credential —
(so goes the heavy promise)
whatever sons authentic are begotten
of Christ's fruitwood and blood.

12

St. Aloysius, Similar to Fire
1568–1591

St. Aloysius grew up in the often treacherous and abusive atmosphere of the notorious Gonzaga family of northern Italy. He was a lotus rising from this silt: a true child prodigy in the areas of asceticism and contemplation. Fiercely independent and protective of these gifts, he found a safe place in the youthful Society of Jesus, where he flowered and then died at the age of twenty-three. —WHM

~

St. Aloysius Gonzaga

Many biographers of Aloysius, it would seem, came to their task afflicted with a strong dose of disbelief. Or at least of half-belief. How could it arrive, they speculate, that such a pure spirit, so unwavering an advocate of the ill and dying, such a paragon of every virtue, such a...etc., could be born to our "bent world"?

This for a start, this semidisbelief; it is like a soil in which spring various fantasies, necromancies, signs, and wonders. And inevitably, we wince, are distanced, disconnected.

In short, such writings imply distrust of the Incarnation in all its surprise and vitality and tripping up of tedious "things as they are." And in dire consequence, the human is all but lost in favor of the superhuman.

A pity, an enormous loss.

◆

For such as Aloysius our need is grave; for someone in our midst, leading the common life, teaching us by example (he being no great

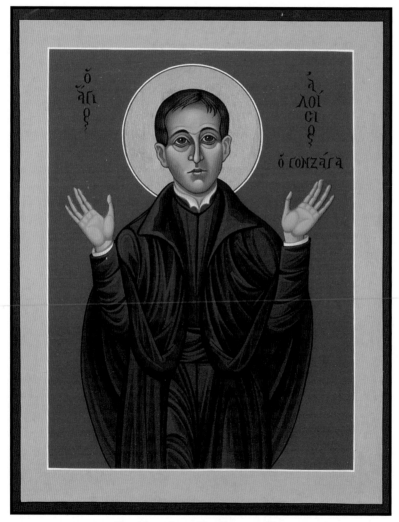

St. Aloysius, Similar to Fire

purveyor of words, let alone of homilies) what we so lack and so need
to know and to do. To live humanly, fully, for others; and this even
when (as currently) public example is singularly unpromising in its
inhumanity, selfishness, greed, violence.

Our need, grave indeed.

And lo! in a maze we lose him.

It is as though Aloysius were not born of our race, were concocted
of another, of elements foreign to the flesh, perhaps of fire and ice,
or night and fog.

As though he cared little for his family and friends, and shut them
from his life, in favor of something amorphously (and famously) known
as "the spiritual life." As though once safe from the world, behind the
walls of a religious community, he took delight in irritating oddities, in
unnerving bouts of prayer and penance.

As though, as though . . . And it is all a charade.

In the first place, in the Jesuit structure and rule, "walls of a religious
community" have no place or pride of metaphor. Quite the opposite;
monastic walls are pulled down. The Jesuits are iconoclasts of immuni-
ties, protections, distancings. They are the original nonmonastics (even
while, in a tribute to the most austere of orders, they hold Carthusians
in special reverence). They renounce orders of the day, set disciplines,
lengthy prayer, and the standing symbols of these — walls, sanctuaries,
cloisters.

Among the most victimized of saints, Aloysius is overlaid with a massive *pentimento*. It renders him all but impervious to starts of affection
and the common plod of life.

And inevitably a question arises. How did the youth cope with the
tight knit of Jesuit life, which might be clumsily put as a form of "being-
as-belonging"? Did he allow his heart to be heard from?

Among Jesuits then as now friendship comes easily; they are great
ones for palaver with one another and with "externs," as well as for
the emoluments of front parlors.

How came it then, the above conceded, that the story of Aloysius has
been so twisted out of joint, a cold charade of a heartwarming reality?

◆

Perhaps a bit of history is in order.

The Jesuits broke an older model of communal Christian life, a model that had stood intact for a thousand years, since Benedict gathered his hermits into cenobitic hives.

Then and later, every genuine innovation depended on a vision. Such was granted Ignatius early on, fittingly enough at a way station. He was en route to Rome, seeking approval for the blueprints of his order. He paused in prayer, and the heavens erupted.

Jesus appeared, we are told, bearing the cross. And along with the Savior, the Father. Ignatius and his disciples were commended to Jesus (it bears repeating) by very God. The task was set forth in a kind of celestial cursive; Jesuits were to heft the cross as had Jesus. Precisely, to be a company of crossbearers.

The vision must be underscored. It was pivotal, on its hinges the future would open. And it came at a price.

It demanded a radical revision of ancient suppositions. Down went the walls. Revealed was an all but impossibly altruistic, vulnerable, even worldly version of faith — of those resolved to live and act and die as public figures, in concert and consequence.

Simple, daring: the stakes of the new order were placed, for weal and woe, in this world — in its ambiguity and darkness, its vagaries and guile, its treacherous caducity. In the world of the Fall, in short.

Thus Jesuits were, in a sense, cast adrift. But hardly as drifters. They had in hand a compass, a map.

Granted, there was small protection, no buffer against the rude tides of fortune — no monastic prayer in common, no cloister, no vows of stability in place or time.

Something else, something unprecedented. The members were to be a species of world-wanderers. Their sole credential was a mandate: go where directed, observe, announce the Word, report back.

At their disposal were sacrament and prayer and mutual affection and an obedience that hemmed in the heart, that declared boundaries and taboos, mainly against intemperate zeal or (equally intemperate) fear and trembling.

◆

Came knocking at the Jesuit door, a neophyte, Aloysius, to the manor born.

Alas, nobility of birth hardly spelled an unmixed blessing. What a scabious tribe, how unsavory their behavior! All but impossible to exaggerate the violence and rapacity, the malfunctioning of wealth and pride of place that surrounded his childhood. In a series of bloody frays, two of his brothers were murdered. Poison, intrigue flowed thick, the blood and murk of a very court of Macbeth.

Aloysius, one reflects somberly, knew himself to the hilt, knew the sheath he was drawn from.

No wonder then, his describing himself as a "piece of twisted iron much in need of straightening!"

◆

From his first years the straightening was underway — guardian angels shadowed him. In 1585, he received his first communion at the hands of St. Charles Borromeo. And once a Jesuit, Aloysius gained for professor another saint, the perspicacious, impossibly learned Robert Bellarmine.

Meantime "No Time Lost" became the Aloysian mantra. He signed away a princely patrimony in favor of his younger brother. Then, his father's disfavor roaring like a contrary wind, he walked away.

As for the Jesuits, a kind of measured improvisation was in the air. The novitiate completed, Aloysius was dispatched posthaste to studies of philosophy and theology.

He survived changes of verve and style, this noble turned commoner. His prayer grew in intensity and depth. In accord with the ethos of the order, union with Christ led further (inevitably one thinks in this young life) to self-giving unto death.

The end of his heartbreakingly brief sojourn neared. He was twenty-three years old when the plague struck Rome. One marvels at the prodigality of the order, which blessed his activity, even as it left him exposed to immanent danger.

His companions dubbed him *il nostro generalino*, "our young general," this most promising of neophytes, his future golden with promise.

◆

No such future was granted. Another "rich young man" turned a page, turned the gospel story around. In the last weeks of Aloysius, the piece of twisted iron glowed and was beaten straight under the hammer blows of providence.

How say our thanks — to him, to that awful Smith we name Christ?

◆

Thanks for this; all unknowing, Aloysius charted a course.

He was a forerunner; more than three thousand Jesuits of later times died as he died, martyrs for the faith or servants of the ill and disfavored.

St. Aloysius, Similar to Fire

Fiery resolve!
A youth in a fiery furnace,
unconsumed,
counsels his soul:
"In this world we burn and burn;
time, place, our purgatorio."

Unconsumed, aflame —
inexplicable, the soul's substance.
"How this portent, how came he to be?
At prayer, he seemed pure spirit;
and when by urging of elders,
alit with compassion, he beheld
the stricken of plague —
see how those arms, *orante*,
took up the cross's sweet burden
and followed, followed after!"

13

Holy Martyrs St. Peter the Aleut and St. Andrew Bobola, S.J.

A Prayer for Unity

In 1815 a young native of Kodiak Island became the third martyr for the Orthodox faith in America when he was tortured and murdered by Roman Catholics, near Mission Dolores in San Francisco, because he would not abandon his faith. His Aleut name was Cungagnaq, but he received the Christian name Peter when he was baptized by the monks of the Kodiak mission.

Father Andrew Bobola was born in 1591 in Poland. He entered the Society of Jesus in Vilna, in 1611. He became an outstanding preacher and catechist, and he also worked amid plagues that struck Vilna in 1624 and 1629. In May of 1657 Cossacks attacked the city of Janow and massacred Catholics and Jews. Andrew Bobola was threatened with death if he would not apostasize. On May 16, Father Bobola was taken by the Cossacks, tortured, and murdered. Like Peter the Aleut, he died a most horrible yet heroic death. — WHM

St. Peter the Aleut and St. Andrew Bobola

Hands in subtle interplay.
Unity is the theme, the circle drawn close.
Blood, coin of the Realm.

Left hand of Andrew, right hand of Peter
all but touching; friends.
Close held at breast, right hand of Andrew,

Holy Martyrs St. Peter the Aleut and St. Andrew Bobola, S.J.

left hand of Peter,
    like the concave rim
of an ample bowl, as though two hearts
in freehold
held.

    Grasped at breast, planted there,
the cross,
Orthodox, Roman.
Two crosses, one Christ.

Plant the cross, in living flesh?

Blood, payment, coin of the Realm.

14

St. Benedict Joseph Labre
1748–1783

St. Benedict Joseph Labre is the patron of the homeless and of those lost in every way. He is also a saint of "extreme humility." In this image he is shown in the symbolic darkness of his "cell" in the Colosseum of Rome, burning with the light of his prayer. —WHM

∾

A saint who, as a young man, knocked at the door of monastery after monastery, Trappist and Carthusian, trying every conventional, communitarian way to holiness.

The monks, it seemed, all admired him — yet no one wanted him. The problem was recurring poor health (which might have been a psychological nudge, "try elsewhere," since later he was to survive far greater rigors than those that spiked the cloister).

There came discouragement: Where does a young aspirant belong in the world, where indeed in the church (which is the dominant form of his world, his only world)? And all the "rest" — the enticements, longings, appetites — do they count for mere dross to a single mind and search?

There followed a moment, a movement of spirit, inexplicable to any human measure or logic. From darkness to light, from uncertainty to a (for his age and time) strangely purposeful resolve.

We learn of it long after the fact, after the honors and invocations and images of holiness. And we wonder at the raw consistency of youth, the all-but-ruthless follow-through.

So no cloister would receive him? None would; the monastic life was a receding dream, a succession of closing doors; thank you but no thank you.

St. Benedict Joseph Labre

Then he would construct a cloister for himself, an itinerant cloister to be sure, and he a gyrovague monk, destitute as a stone of the road, his feet bare, his purse empty, and he bound for — everywhere.

"Everywhere" was no idle dream or nirvana. "Everywhere" was the claim he staked in virtue of a breakthrough, places that belonged in this world only by the incursion of another world. Everywhere, to be understood as this or that sanctuary where the Sanctus had broken through, where Jesus or Mary or one of the saints had vouchsafed an epiphany among humans.

Wherever (to be practical, to ground this highly charged, spontaneous combustion of grace, this matter of young Benedict Joseph, his vagrancy, his nonstatus in church and world) — wherever there was a Mass to be celebrated or an advocate to be invoked.

A simple enough rule: be there, belong there, pray, vigil, and pass on.

The program, and its setting. An old coat, a rosary around his neck, a crucifix at his breast. In a sack a New Testament, a breviary, a copy of the *Imitation of Christ*. He would sleep on the ground, would eat chance leftovers. As to monies, nothing of security; he would take alms when offered, give away everything beyond bare need.

It was daring, appallingly so. It was also dangerous, on many counts. Benedict would be like a Jew in Babylon, without companion or community or sanctified rule or means of sustenance.

His resolve would be called, in the jargon of our day, "recessive." In plain fact he was dramatizing the "birds of the air and foxes of the field," invoked negatively by his Savior. Fauna indeed have their proper place, their "nests and holes." Jesus, for his part, has neither. He chooses a place, a status in the scheme of things, beneath the lowliest of the living.

How daring, how dangerous! How easily this "experiment in extremes" could founder, make wreckage of the pilgrim, grind his purpose to pieces on the world's millstones — which then as now, grind exceedingly fine!

◆

Rebecca West, reflecting on a meeting with D. H. Lawrence, offers a hint of analogous purpose:

There seemed no reason why he had made these journeys, which were all as uncomfortable as cheap traveling is in Italy; nor did there seem to be any reason why he was presently going to Baden-Baden. Yet if every word he said disclosed less and less reason for this journeying, it all disclosed a very definite purpose. These were the journeys that the mystics of a certain type have always found necessary. The Russian saint goes to the head of his family and says good-bye and takes his stick and walks out with no objective but the truth. The Indian fakir draws lines with his bare feet across the dust of his peninsula which describe a diagram meaningless to the uninitiated, but significant of holiness.

Lawrence traveled, it seemed, to get a certain Apocalyptic vision of humankind which he registered again and again and again, always rising to a pitch of ecstatic agony. . . . We knew that what he was doing was right. We nodded and were entranced.

"The Russian saint goes to the head of his family and says good-bye and takes his stick and walks out. . . . " Uncanny, exact. So did the French saint. His purpose was plain — to him, if to no other.

Plain to God? So the church has declared.

Benedict set out, in the first instance, for Italy. From Piedmont (from, one thinks, that safe distance), he wrote his father a letter. The traditional farewell of a holy fool? In any case, a last exchange between the two. He cut the cord.

In the first seven years, he journeyed to the great shrines of western Europe: to Italy, Switzerland, Spain, France.

Six years remained to him. He settled, if one can use an inexact word, in Rome. There the essentials of his "rule" were faithfully kept: destitution and prayer. He slept in the Colosseum, quite at home it would seem, among the felines prowling about the ruins. His days were spent in visiting the great churches.

And then in Lent of 1783, he died. And the word went about the city like an electric charge: "The saint is dead!" He would have disclaimed the honor that followed; but after all, he was safe, being dead.

◆

St. Benedict Joseph Labre

Appearances, semblances;
one sees his like
anywhere on earth today.

Stress: "today";
Stress: "appearances."
We require an image
speaking to the inner ear
through outer eye —
a Candle Flame,
a Hand from a Cloud.

We require a gift.
In the ancient scrolls: Wisdom.
Or: attentiveness, vigilance,
the third eye of mindfulness.

Implied here
something of urgent moment;
a biblical version —
        ourselves,
who we are in the world,
where bound.

The icon:
the attention of Benedict Joseph
is elsewhere;
        on the Candle Flame
blown about, endangered —
the winds of the world fierce blowing.

Attention:
        a mysterious
disembodied Hand
        reaches out — as though
                an act of creation.
Attention! Elsewhere!

Love is other than
the lover's eyes
    meeting the eye of the beloved;
no, love is the eye of each
turned in the same direction!

The Candle illumines the way.
The way, the becoming, the never arriving —
trudging toward, not giving up —

Benedict Joseph —
your strange, uncharted pilgrimage!
prayer in holy places,
candles kept alight,
interventions, that
Cloud of Unknowing.
All this and more —
literal, taking to heart the text,
"Blessed the poor in spirit,
the reign of God is theirs."

The words pierce
"to the joining place of bone and marrow";

and this, in a pitiful
"century of accretion,"
the quality, scope,
accumulation, glitter,
sham beginning to show —

these build
a ladder to the stars.
Rung by rung the rich mount,
credentials irrefutable;
great possessions.

Someone refuses, turns away
(turns toward the Candle,
the Cloud, the Hand),
discrediting the charade.

No. "Blessed are the poor."

See
those on the ladder of gold
supported, sustained
by the poor.
    Some few
mounting the ladder of gold.
        A multitude
support, sustain, uphold.

No more of this!
From someone, a gesture,
a sublime contempt.
Someone refusing
to hold the ladder steady,
refusing
the meager coins, falling
from on high.

Holding the ladder steady —
a static gesture.
Implied:
a kind of numb despair,
closure of alternatives.

Benedict walked away.
        Hands
have better tasks.
    Feet: walk.

He "withdrew support."

And the ladder?
It swayed where it stood.

    A few high and mighty,
      a multitude upholding things,
and Benedict, refuser.

And the "system"
    was not, after all,
firmly planted, eternal, credible, honorable, inevitable!
    Not,
    not "the divine will."

Benedict walked away.
    Toward. Walked toward.
    He walked toward.
Human lo! on pilgrimage.

    And time —
a plod, free, creaturely,
against odds to be sure,
        joyous, yes
    toward —

    a holy place
the Candle will show, the Hand beckon!

15

St. Maria Goretti
1890–1902

The saints are like the New Testament prophets, and their acts are the continuation of a book that will close only with the return of the Lord. Maria Goretti surfaces over and over in our culture as a stumbling block and witness.

Maria is the "prematurely old child" bearing heavy responsibilities because of deaths in her family and the family's subsequent poverty. Maria is the "radiant child" bearing a dignity and prayerfulness beyond her years — her life being one that would attract both good and evil. Maria is the "abused child" determined to protect herself while being worn down, stalked, and threatened by a family friend. Finally, Maria is a Christ figure, forgiving from her death bed, forgiving the unforgivable . . . a sign and symbol of the flowering cross.   —WHM

⇜

Virtue knows both good and evil;
evil, only itself.
The rule, but for grace of God,
is ironbound.

    But grace is a fire
wherein plunged,
      iron, unbound, learns
under hammer blows, new shape and scope!

Maria, slum child,
burdened beyond her years, knowing
good and evil conflicted.
    She chose, and closed a door.

St. Maria Goretti

Evil bode its time.
She died in blood, this tender child.

In the icon, a child
as though imagined by a child.
Two hands, workaday, weary,
like weathered sticks
crossed at breast,
modest, self-protective,
reverential.
Her eyes burn with "Why?"

No turning aside, not
for a moment.
Not from us.
Not from her murderer,
from her mourners.
Not from the children.

Hair falls in a cascade
black, red, livid, thick as hemp
roped with blood.
Clothing — crimson,
dyed in blood.

The knife is raised.
Maria, child,
falls in blood.

The year, 1902. She is
portal and portent,
emblem of a bloodshot century.

Maria, first of the children of war,
children of sanctions,
children unwanted,
children aborted,
children falling to hunger,
children tortured and disappeared.

St. Maria, pray for us.

16

The Servant of God
Benjamin Joseph Salmon

1889–1932

Ben Salmon was born to a working-class Catholic family in Denver in 1889. From his youth he was given by the Holy Spirit a radical longing for the nonviolent message of Jesus Christ in the gospel, and the courage to bear this calling. These values were in terrible conflict with his times, yet he remained a devout Catholic.

When called to participate in World War I, Salmon applied for conscientious objector status but was rejected because the church had long ago formulated a "just war" theory. He was arrested in 1918, sentenced to death, then twenty-five years in prison. His sufferings in prison were compounded by his decision to go on an indefinite hunger strike in protest. When the authorities tired of force-feeding him, Salmon was released from prison in 1920. Salmon's pacifism contradicted the moral theologians of his time, and he leaned on the early church and the witness of the Christian martyrs who gave their lives to oppose the idolatry of the Roman Empire. His health impaired by his ordeal, he died at the age of forty-three in 1932. —WHM

He brings to mind the buried treasure of the gospel story, this unlikely hero.

He was born in an unlikely city, Denver, Colorado.

How could he know that one day its resident critics would unite in scoring him, with a great groan of the media, as a "drone," an "arch slacker," a "violent anti-war CO," a "man with a yellow streak down his spine"...?

His crime? He was anti-Denver, anti-American, even anti-Catholic. He was antiwar. He was guilty of the Great Refusal.

The year was 1914; the country was embarking on Wilson's "war to end all wars." And in the bastion of busbies, Salmon dared, cannily, with more than a soupçon of irony, to put his convictions on record: "If killing has to be insisted on, those responsible for wars — kings, presidents, kaisers, etc. — should be made to fight each other and not drag millions of innocent youths into a game where they would be compelled to slaughter each other." Outrageous. The reaction was swift: Was it not wartime? Were Catholics not bound (one thinks of the survival instinct of an immigrant people and the bidding of their religious authorities) — bound to follow the flag?

Ben was summarily ejected from the Knights of Columbus, a fraternal organization famed for its tightfisted Catholic Americanism.

Worse was to come. Imprisoned for refusing induction, Ben encountered a number of priests, chaplains to the military. One after another, each fired off an ecclesiastical salvo. This solitary prisoner was demented or ethically awry, or both; the church would grant him no concession, allow him no sacrament.

In many details, Ben's story eerily resembles that of an Austrian counterpart, Franz Jägerstätter, and his resistance against World War II. Both were working-class married men, had fathered children. Both were Catholic. Both were repudiated by the church. Both were offered alternate noncombatant service by their governments, and refused the concession.

Their decision to resist war worked hardship on their families: spouses endured public odium; children were raised and educated as best the women could, alone.

Jägerstätter was finally executed. Salmon, too, was condemned to death, a sentence afterward commuted to twenty-five years at hard labor.

On November 11, 1918, the armistice was signed. The war to end all wars was over, but Ben's sentence had scarcely begun.

In a private war of wills, he was shuttled about the country from one military gulag to another: from Fort Logan, Colorado, to Camp Funston, Kansas; to Camp Dodge, Iowa; then back to Kansas and an ominous phase at Fort Leavenworth.

The Servant of God Benjamin Joseph Salmon

There was no bargaining with him; he was baffling, outrageous, iron-willed. He was Irish. No, he would not work for "our natural butchering process, ... the system." "To work in a military prison is to aid the killing machine." And yes, he would organize a strike, to protest "the larceny of funds" designated for prisoners' food.

In wit and wisdom he could be devastating: "I would rather be one of the conscientious objectors who died in the stand for genuine Christianity, than to be wearing a breast full of medals for service rendered the devil on fields of battle."

Today, more than thirty years after his death, his writings offer an anthology of riches. Suffering lent a razor's edge to the mind of this "uneducated" working man.

Thus, he countered a Jesuit ethician who defended in print the just war theory: "Either Christ is a liar or war is never necessary; and, very properly assuming that Christ told the truth, it follows that the state is without judicial authority to determine when war is necessary — because it is never necessary."

No giving in. A further punishment, another circle of hell was devised for him — bread and water and solitary confinement. Catholic chaplains, exasperated, tarred him as "recalcitrant" and "reckless." Six months of this. Released to the prison population, he remained adamant; not a finger lifted, no working for the system.

His logic was delicious. He saw concession as a game of dominoes falling: "If I could work five minutes, I could work a day, and if I could work a day, I could work a year, and if I could work a year, I could join the army...."

Off again he was trundled. He was the original patron of holy gyrovagues, a Saint Elsewhere. The destination this time: Fort Douglas, Utah. He arrived in shackles.

No, he would not work.

Threatened again, this time with life imprisonment, his response was typical, uncowed. He put it in writing: the commandant could "have me tried by court-martial immediately and give me a million years in sentences; but I would not go to work."

The war had come home, as wars will. The brutalities of the battle-fields spilled over, a domestic witches' brew. He and his companions tasted it. He reported, "Starvation, beatings, cold baths in zero weather, bayoneting, were the order of the day." Later he added, summing up, and in spite of all, exulting: "Every method of torture was used, and while many died, only a few were broken in spirit."

The armistice was declared. More than a year passed. And Salmon and the other COs remained in prison.

Hell on earth, being the work of humans, must be endlessly reinvented. For these refusers, new circles within circles were drawn up.

Ben took to evaluating his past, with a view toward a further act of resistance. He recalled how at the start, he had refused to report for induction. He would not work at assigned tasks or wear a military uniform. He resisted the official theft of prisoners' food money.

The war ended. And here he sat, under lockup. Prison, that bitter pill, stuck in his throat. Was this to be borne? Everything indicated a further step.

On July 17, 1920, Salmon announced his decision: he was undertaking a hunger strike "for liberty or for death."

Christ's urging that we "overcome evil with good," he wrote, is "the most effective solution for individual and societary [*sic*] ills...ever formulated."

He was at the brink. "My life, my family, everything is now in the hands of God. His will be done." Though under duress, he could be dauntingly logical in reflecting on his decision. He writes in the tone of Dorothy Day:

> We do not attempt to overcome lying with lies; we overcome it with truth. We do not try to overcome curses with curses, but we overcome with silence or with words of friendship....
>
> Sickness is not overcome with sickness; it is overcome with health. If I cut my finger, the remedy is not to cut another finger, but to succor the original wound. Anger is overcome by meekness, pride by humility.

And he comes to the nub of his argument: "The successful way to overcome the evil of war is by the good of peace, a steadfast refusal to 'render evil for evil.'"

No food, no water, indefinitely.

Another military chaplain entered his cell. This one too proved a harrier of our Job. The priest pontificated; Salmon's hunger strike was "suicidal" and a "mortal sin."

Salmon was unmoved. And inevitably, official anger flared anew. They were at wit's end with him.

He was shipped out again, this time on a daunting continental trek. It was an instance of military overkill, with armed guards, a train with drawn shades, a physician, a commandant — all this to control a single prisoner, half-dead with fasting.

What were they to do with this baffling subverter?

The prisoner's train sped out of Utah eastward.

Ben was deposited, under lock and key, in St. Elizabeth's Mental Hospital in Washington, D.C. In the blueprint of hell, a further circle had been devised. It included a dwelling of sorts for the otherwise unclassifiable.

Salmon was classified, once for all, locked in a wing of the hospital set apart for the "criminally insane."

He had been thrust in each of hell's circles, rejecting such, declaring with a sublime perversity that this or that cell was ill-fitted to his needs. Which is to say, to his conscience.

A hospital for the insane, a scene of cacophony and anguish. His report:

> The wilder ones rave and holler, all day long they rant and screech, sometimes in stentorian tones, sometimes a little milder.
>
> ...At night everyone is perfectly quiet except for the intermittent ravings of various unfortunates and the innocent conversations of those who seem to have many friends conversing with them in their solitary cells.

Salmon had arrived at hell's home address.

He continued his strike for an unprecedented eighty days. For months, he was force-fed several times each day. But ever so slowly, a tide was gathering. Support for the resister grew, even in the Catholic Church.

The military mind, let it be suggested, reasons somewhat like this: when a tactic proves useless, repeat it. Ben was shipped off once more, from hell to purgatory, so to speak. To Walter Reed Military Hospital. It was the last redoubt of an astonishing survivor.

In November 1920, signed, sealed, and delivered to Benjamin Joseph Salmon was a dishonorable discharge from the U.S. Army. Hell had given up its prey.

Peacemaking exacted of Ben Salmon a terrifying price, just short of the fate of Franz Jägerstätter.

They could not defeat Salmon. But the fasting, the torment of force-feeding, the solitary caging, fell on him like a hundredweight, shortening his life.

In the harsh Chicago winter of 1932, in his forty-third year, he fell ill with pneumonia and within days, died.

◆

See, brutes huff and puff,
they rake the world with fire,
they build hecatombs
of shuddering bones.

The God of life
half-attentive,
keeps them at edge of eye;
no need of
vengeance, of judgment;
they crumble,
a faulty tower
down wind!

At center eye
the apple of God's eye
blossoms, swells, ripens —
the faithful who fall
straight as a plumb line
into
God's right hand!

                    (after Psalm 33)

17

The Servant of God Adrienne von Speyr

1902–1967

"Medical doctor, mystical writer, stigmatic . . . born into one of Basel's oldest families and schooled in the Protestant tradition. A three-year bout with tuberculosis preceded her study of medicine. She worked her way through medical school to become a doctor in 1928. In 1927 she married Emil Durr. . . . His death in 1934 drove her to the brink of suicide. In 1936 she married Werner Kagi. . . . She maintained a busy practice, seeing up to 80 patients a day. . . . Her meeting with Hans Urs von Balthasar, in the fall of 1940, then chaplain at the University of Basel, and her subsequent conversion to Catholicism ended the quest which had thus far characterized her inner life. . . .

"The defenseless availability of the mystic makes possible a perfect obedience to God and to her confessor. . . . Meditative commentaries on the Bible make up a major portion of von Speyr's work, reflecting her conviction that Christian mysticism necessarily proceeds from Holy Scripture" (The Catholic Encyclopedia, s.v. Adrienne von Speyr).

A great number of the icons in this book were commissions, which are always challenging work. Every so often I would stop with the list of commissions and paint someone I felt drawn to, like Adrienne von Speyr, Ben Salmon, or Francisco Marto of Fátima. Adrienne von Speyr speaks with authority. It can be a shock to read her work at first — she is so surgical and bold.   —WHM

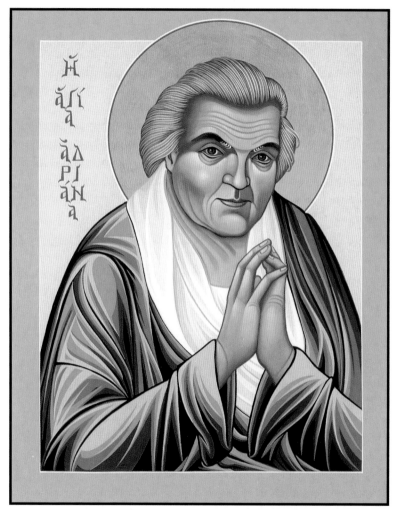

The Servant of God Adrienne von Speyr

A passing glance in the direction of this life, and a thought occurs. A rather remarkable woman, surely, but always within limits: the limits of Swiss bourgeoisie, of a certain solidity of temperament, of competent professional skills.

Conceded, she is independent of mind, will, when required, step out of rank. Thus she enters medical school, that male enclave jealously guarded. Once settled in her profession, she proves energetic, anxious to prove herself. Incalculable energies! She works night and day on behalf of the ill.

◆

She is also religiously devout. (We are still indulging first thoughts.) Influenced by a famous Jesuit. She converts from the Lutheran Church to Catholicism. The event raises eyebrows; it is rather unusual but by no means unheard of in her circle and time.

◆

The above might be judged a first glance, rather superficial, directed at a remarkable life.

Adrienne actually plunges us into deeper waters. If we merely ride the surface, she appears as a modern phenomenon; admirable but hardly unique. A woman who marries, starts a family, attains professional status (how easily such words are set down, with small attention to the price exacted of a woman, making her way as best she might in a male enclave!).

◆

Then, as one pays attention, what marvels appear: an astonishingly gifted interior life.

A life within a life: a missive, her soul, a message signed, sealed, sent off — to God. (And its envelope, a doctor's life, its passion and compassion. The ill crowding into her dispensary, the self-giving year after year. This and marriage, family, children.)

◆

She is a visionary — and this at six years of age!

At Christmastime in 1908, she wrote years later, a man came toward her on the street, taking her hand:

> He appeared poor and limped a bit. At first I was really frightened; then he started to look at me and said, "I thought you would come with me; won't you?" . . . With a sense of fear I replied, "No Sir, but merry Christmas." He immediately let go of my hand; he seemed to me a bit sad. . . . I kept saying over and over again to myself, "Perhaps I should have said yes, but I could not."

It was the first of many visions. And how ironic: she, a Lutheran child, visited by the great Counter-Reformation figure, Ignatius Loyola!

The ironies hardly are exhausted by the event itself. The saint who beckons her, who "takes her hand," is anonymous; she recognizes him only years later.

She will live out a generous span of life, professionally absorbed in the sufferings of others, writing copious mystical theology, visited repeatedly by Mary, Thérèse of Lisieux, the Curé of Ars, Ignatius. Unexplained healings occur and are widely noticed. She is subject to a series of "Passions," experiencing the inner sufferings of Jesus; after Holy Week of 1942 she receives the wounds of the Savior on her body.

◆

She was careful and discreet, as a doctor must be. The "visitations" were never spoken about, except to one person, her friend and counselor. In him she was lucky; the priest encouraged her at every point, and in time became a kind of amanuensis, the Jesuit theologian Hans Urs von Balthasar.

A supremely sensible woman, one thinks; a doctor of body, and of spirit as well.

As she well knows, charisms do not exist in a vacuum of time or place; they are granted in view of the welfare of others.

◆

Could not her lifelong love of scripture, her supple, piercing exegesis, itself be a form of charism? She wrote or dictated twenty-seven volumes of commentary!

And those strange "visits" of hers. Of them von Balthasar writes:

> She loved the word and the reality of "being available," an ex-
> pression which appears repeatedly in her books. God took her at
> her word and during the hours of prayer that filled her nights, He
> often allowed her to "travel" in ever new ways.
>
> She was "transported" in prayer to countless places where
> her praying, helping presence was needed; during the War, into
> concentration camps...
>
> Even in the final weeks of her fatal illness, she referred to
> having "traveled" in this way.

Love and competence and stunning insights into the Word of God —
and then those strange "travels."

◆

And one thinks of a mystery, the mystery of goodness permeating,
transfiguring the mystery of evil.

Adrienne must be wherever Christ is denied or played down or
outright mocked; worse, where the drama of his death is enacted again.

◆

"Even as a small child," writes von Balthasar, "she had always experienced joy when it was mentioned that she might die." Death came
after protracted illness, on September 17, 1967.

◆

Death no dominion. In her last days Adrienne gave death a new face,
all light and resurrection. "How beautiful it is to die!" she said.

As the end approached, the wounds of Christ disappeared from
her body.
◆

Adrienne von Speyr

> "Unassuming"; the word
> captures like a cunning net's
> free fall, Adrienne.
> Her hands join fitly in prayer.

"To clasp one's hands in prayer
is the beginning
of an uprising
against the disorder of the world." (Karl Barth)

Eyes alert,
    hair springing to an aureole,
face full as a full moon,
robed in ample blue.
    Her glance
falls within, without;
    hands empty — only herself
to offer.

Enough.
Sated with charlatan claimants, we know it; enough —
substance, clarity.

But for herself, enough?
    For such as her,
        as Clare, as Padre Pio,
as Teresa of Ávila,
    as Ignatius — never enough.
"She realized" (writing of St. Clare)
"contemplation is mother of action."
And again of Clare: "She becomes in prayer
a young lover."

Of St. Elizabeth of Hungary: "And now
she begins. Her anxious caution
is blown away.
There is one possible answer to God —
the entirety, everything!"

And then, receiving the wounds of Christ
in hands and feet —
a charming image.
She summons St. Francis:

"As if the wounds of the Lord
had accidentally fallen
like two rose petals into his hands,
while he was contemplating a rosebush.
As if the petals served
only to help him
better to contemplate roses."

18

The Servant of God
Egide Van Broeckhoven, S.J.
1933–1967

Egide was a hidden light of the inspired movement of "worker priests." He kept a diary of his spiritual life and vocation, "to teach people the mystical depths of friendship." Egide was killed in a factory accident December 28, 1967. —WHM

~

The words of Egide:

I want to become a person only by searching and visiting God.

It seems there is no one today who is sure of the right choice; the structures which once inspired blind trust (school, church) are placed in doubt. We have been driven into a corner where we are face-to-face with what is essential.

When we think of God creating, we think of a mythical past or a sacred future. But it is a joy to discover that this mythical and sacred creation is the very concrete world of the here and now; in this place and at this time in Brussels, these workmen in this greasy foundry, our friends too; all this is reality and this reality is sacred, because it is the only situation through which God can reach us. . . . If I had to choose between the burning bush and Brussels, I'd choose Brussels.

Our first duty is not to proclaim the history of salvation . . . but first of all to be a bit of that history ourselves. . . . I cannot, I must not, go back on my decision to become a worker-priest.

The Servant of God Egide Van Broeckhoven, S.J.

He chose (and was chosen for, as he firmly believed) a mode of life: a factory worker. The job got underway.

And then the young priest died.

"What a waste!" is a first thought. A man of "another class" enters the forbidding bleak world of factories. He is short of robust. Yet physical stamina and a measure of emotional hardening are absolute requirements for survival. The work is brutal, the workers rough and ready.

As for the priest, he is ludicrously inept. Fired from one job as an incompetent, on his second try he is all thumbs, and stumbles into this or that mischance. He would be dismissed today as "accident prone."

But there are other sides to the story, pointing in a different direction. He is a persistent diary-keeper. Night after night he mulls over life and its mischances, transmitting his clumsy gestures by a stubborn vision.

The second mitigating circumstance was the affection Egide's fellow workers showed him. No matter the rough talk and religious indifference (or even hostility) — their hearts warmed to this little priest, somewhat frail, eager to listen to them, to please and be of use.

Theirs was no demeaning pity for him; something better.

He won their hearts by offering them his own. He had an extraordinary gift for friendship. This was the soul of his spirituality, this reaching out to his fellows, victimized as they were by the clutch of the almighty dollar. Ignored also and shrugged off by the church.

Then one day his story came to a halt. In a horrendous accident the priest Egide died, instantly, on the job, slammed to a wall by huge metal plates. He was thirty-four years old.

So short a life, so banal a death?

Still there is that vision to be taken into account.

A vision. It made of absurdity a lofty irrefutable logic, an "equal" sign.

It linked another supreme Waste, another Death, with his own. "Kenotic" is the word, St. Paul's. He would name this Egide as an embodiment of the Incarnation of God. Everything given, nothing left over.

The Christ of emptied veins would understand. And we Christians — how can we not grow more thoughtful?

19

Holy Priest, Anonymous One of Sachsenhausen

February 1940

*This icon of an anonymous priest murdered in 1940 at the concentra-
tion camp in Sachsenhausen — the camp in Germany to which most
gay men were sent — is inspired by an eyewitness account by Heinz
Heger in his book* The Men with the Pink Triangle. *— WHM*

∾

Unknown Prisoner of Sachsenhausen

*The apparent absence of the Almighty leads us back to His presence.
His absence is the mark of His presence. Divine absence in our time
has two forms. One is the threat of the abyss. . . . The other is the new
technology of death presented by the death camps. To think religion
through is to rediscover the holy in-between and in-spite-of, this double
negation. . . . God draws a curtain of darkness down before Himself in
order to allow light to appear, darkness serving as the necessary foil for
illumination.* — Carolyn Forché, Against Forgetting

No wonder the author of the Letter to the Hebrews named them only
as a "cloud of witnesses" — named them, that is, only as far as he
was able.

Not very far to be sure, for the writer was only human; and the Word
of God pressed on him, lest he break limits. According to that Word,
these are to remain essentially nameless, declared such by the powers
of this world, who would well be rid of them.

Holy Priest, Anonymous One of Sachsenhausen

Not only claiming their lives, but denying them existence. This is the triumph of what Oscar Romero called the "security state": to deny their existence. As in the death camps a sign might well proclaim, "We don't know whom you're talking about. They were never here." The technique of the ovens all but wiped them out, dust and ashes and all.

The technique went further; if the victims never existed, it follows that no crime can be adduced, no guilt implied. If no records remain regarding the fate of such as Gypsies, Jews, Jesuits, homosexuals, the physically or mentally impaired — then why the outcry?

This, as we have seen, is the final triumph of the massive criminal state apparatus, courts, jails, academics (the law of the land supreme, above conscience or Bible or international law), the courageous brought to heel, the churches gagged. We saw nothing, we heard nothing — therefore we say nothing; there was no crime.

And the victims, that "cloud of witnesses" — their only name, a floating vaporous paladin, vast or tiny, obscuring for a moment or perhaps entire days, the sun.

A "cloud," associated in mystical language with "unknowing," and, one thinks, exactly so. Their names are unknown. We cannot, as the saying goes, "put a face to them." No one steps forward, spouse, lover, sister, friend, son, daughter, to claim them, extol them, tell their story.

At least for a time — perhaps in most instances, for all time.

And the church? On their behalf (on our behalf) the church confesses a kind of helplessness, submits before this sublime anonymity, groups the "witnesses" in a single vast chorus of celebration and triumph. The church summons them, invokes them as mediators before the Throne, one and all nameless, under the rubric of "All Saints."

A sublime paradox lurks here.

It is this estate of enforced humiliation, this namelessness, that grants the dead their greatest dignity: the dignity of the godly. For God, too, is nameless, beyond our knowing or naming. And woe betide the mortal — savant, theologian, or mystic — who sets out on this perilous path into the unknown and unknowable.

The God who knows and names himself also summons the "dry

bones" of desert places. The Spirit breathes; they stand and praise God, who grants existence to that which was not, who knows and names the nameless ones.

The technology of the ovens is quite literally demonic. It reverses, thwarts, the creative act of God, even as it dramatizes the socialized death wish.

This latter implies the nonexistence of the victim ("no records available") and the guiltlessness of an entire imperial machinery, mobilized in favor of an official shrug, a cover-up ("no evidence of crime").

◆

Thus this victim, known from the start as a priest, is one among a multitude of the nameless. Like his captors, a German ("We learned later that he came from Sudetenland, from an aristocratic German family").

And a contrast. Unlike the other prisoners (including the one who tells of him!), the priest is granted a face, a description: "Some sixty years of age, tall and with distinguished features."

Is the detail designed to heighten the pathos of what follows? The stuff of tragedy is prepared; pity and fear stir in us. We are face-to-face with more than a nameless one, with a tradition, a Creon or Oedipus or Laocoon, wound in the coils of — fate?

Let us venture that it was not fate but vocation.

He is called to this. To be hated roundly, above measure, this priest, meriting more than a "normal" dose of malignancy, as the witness records. A "special case," a homosexual, a priest.

A double offense, to be paid for in a kind of double death: public shame, obloquy, physical punishment unto bloodletting, a death slowly exacted.

He dies over hours, days; it is as though a garment, thoroughly cleansed, were being wrung out by hand.

His namelessness is relative; it is relieved, as is that of the author who survived to tell the priest's story. "I had always a great respect for priests," he writes.

And the circle of "the nameless who are named" widens. A multitude of Simons of Cyrene! Many among the prisoners come to the aid of the dying priest. He is beaten and tied to a board. Afterward, "We laid him on his bed." And again, the next morning, "When we marched to the parade-ground, we had almost to carry the priest."

The witness understands the irony, and records it. The priest is nameless, yet his suffering genetically connects him to a Name. And a Name greatly surpassing any name of heaven or earth: "I felt I was witnessing the crucifixion of Christ in modern guise." And this in striking detail: parody, parity, our nameless observer misses nothing. "Instead of Roman soldiers Hitler's SS thugs, and bench instead of the cross."

At the hour of the priest's death, the circle widens further. A multitude of his fellow prisoners are witnesses to a kind of epiphany in nature. It quite stops the horrid show.

Is one perhaps justified in calling the event a "naming at last"?

The prisoners are mustered for roll call. The priest is dying where he stands. His dying is offensive, he slouches, unable to stand erect. Very well then, he will be forced upright, beaten. Then,

> from the overcast sky, a sudden ray of sunshine illuminated the priest's battered face, ... out of thousands of assembled prisoners, only he — and at the moment when he was to be beaten.
>
> There was a remarkable silence; all present stared fixedly at the sky, astonished. ... The SS sergeant looked up in wonder for a few seconds, then his hand, raised for a blow, sank slowly to his side. He walked wordlessly away. ...
>
> The priest bowed his head and murmured with a dying voice, "Thank you, Lord. ... I know my time has come. ... "

Naming Jesus, he was named. By evening he was dead.

◆

Holy Priest, Anonymous One of Sachsenhausen

> "The king ordered that the furnace be stoked
> seven times more than usual. [The three]
> were bound and cast into the white hot furnace
> together with their coats, hats,
> shoes, and other garments,
> for the king's order was urgent.

"So huge a fire was kindled in the furnace
the flames devoured the men
who cast [the three] into it.

"These three fell, bound,
into the white hot furnace."

◆

Anonymous as ashes, the priest
"in the white hot furnace"
bearing at breast the notorious pink triangle,
the sign
       (all scorn scornfully aside)
of Trinitarian life and love.

◆

"Now the king's men who had thrown them in,
continued to stoke the furnace
with brimstone, pitch, tow, and faggots.
The flames rose forty-nine cubits above the furnace
and spread out, burning the Chaldeans nearby.

"But the angel of the Lord
went down into the furnace, . . .
drove the fiery flames out of the furnace
and made the inside . . .
as though a dew-laden breeze were blowing through it."

◆

Sentence of death?
            It touches him not at all.
How could it?
The triune God dwells in him;
unsinged, unharmed, hands aloft, the priest
prays mightily.

The jacket of shame trembles
as though in a firestorm of soul,
     as though fear and ecstasy
          contended for his frame.

     Look how he walks
resolute, straight toward us.

A small matter, soon done with.
     Death no dominion.

20

Holy Martyr Franz Jägerstätter
1907–1943

This young Austrian prophet, husband, father, and member of the Third Order of St. Francis refused to be inducted into Hitler's army and was beheaded on August 9, 1943. —WHM

❧

Through His bitter suffering and death, Christ freed us only from eternal death, not from temporal suffering and moral death. But Christ, too, demands a public confession of our faith, just as the Führer, Adolf Hitler, does from his followers. . . . I am convinced that it is still best that I speak the truth, even if it costs me my life. . . . I cannot and may not take an oath in favor of a government that is fighting an unjust war. . . . I thank you dear Jesus, too, that I am privileged to suffer and even die for Him. . . . The heart of Jesus, the heart of Mary, and my own heart are one, united for time and eternity. Mary with Child so dear, give us all your blessings.
— *Franz Jägerstätter, writing from prison to his wife and children*

Meditation on a Martyr

Born under that murky, ambiguous sign: not a double cross, so to speak, but a bent cross, disabled, tampered with, horribly altered, crooked, nightmarish.

Dare we admit it: this is the cross which (despite all frantic denials) we too are born under? Or the one we create for ourselves? The one we bend around, to our own crooked uses and whims and frenzies.

What we make of the cross!

◆

Holy Martyr Franz Jägerstätter

I would not venture that Franz saw this from the first (who does?) — only that he saw it eventually. That cross hideously altered in form: a cross that favors deception, war-making, unaccountability.

He saw. And he told what he saw. And then he died in witness to what he saw.

What happened to such a one that this occurred? What the preface of his rebirth and then death?

◆

His world was no vacuum; more like a tornado. The chariot of Nazi Germany rolled on like a wheel of fate, the wheels ground to bits whoever, by mischance or heroic purpose, put themselves in the way.

Franz put himself in the way. Not all at once; his was no "great leap forward" (a gesture that more often than not lands in a void). His was a better way, gradual, step by step.

Confusion, then clarity. He was like the blind man in the gospel, drawn slowly out of darkness. He saw not at all; then he saw "men like trees walking." Then he saw.

◆

We see him then, husband and father. He has work now; in the fields, in the church: i.e., is the village sacristan.

Summer, toward midday. The farmers are in the fields, the church is empty. Franz sits there or kneels there, open Bible in hand, quite alone.

He's trying to make sense of a certain text. On the one hand, he sees the words violated or ignored or trivialized all over Austria. This is astonishing, for the text seems simple and clear.

What can it mean, this business of loving enemies, doing good to those who do ill, turning the other cheek, walking the extra mile? His brow is furrowed; he's looking for light in a midnight tunnel.

He gives the words time, a long time. Days, weeks. Eventually he realizes: all this thinking is going nowhere.

Then he starts to let go. And his heart begins to breathe. Now his mind dwells on love. Love that opens doors, opens texts, means what it says, does not counsel lightly, matches words with deeds. And above all, is not fooled, but scrutinizes — the heart, the public situation.

The heart that, so to speak, sees something, then makes up its mind. And follows through.

◆

The text comes to life, but never in a vacuum. Indeed, Austria is under the gun (and loves it, as the wild welcome given Hitler and the plebiscite showed!).

But for Franz, the world is going to very hell. In a tank. In a (newly created) bomber. In a blitzkrieg.

In a racing train, as he saw in a dream.

He saw it, he could never forget it. That train! "All aboard!" sounding, everybody scrambling to climb aboard, to go with what's going. Or as he wrote bluntly (as a voice in his dream said bluntly): To go to hell.

This is appalling, unbearable. Christians are climbing aboard. Priests and bishops. And then the faithful, assured that the ride is free and fast and safe.

What direction can he seek from such a church (a church which he has only of late begun to take seriously)?

But will the church take him seriously?

◆

That train, steaming toward him in the darkness: All aboard for hell! What to do? The burden of asking one's soul, again and again, and with little help from others — what to do?

And what of wife, and what of the children?

◆

His passion was to see things as they are, see Hitler for what he is, take up the gospel, put it on — whole cloth, a second skin.

No slogans could win him over, no command to fall in line. The priests tried, friends tried. But neither church nor state could shunt his conscience around.

The time came, the notice of military induction. And Franz uttered his great, though modest and, at the beginning, generally despised, refusal.

What was the source of that refusal? One could speak of solitude, of steadfastness. Of a purity and clarity of soul no contempt could besmirch.

◆

He was condemned to die; and then to stay dead.

Or so they thought, those who spoke for, or thought for, or opined for, church and state. Not knowing (not believing) that the holy dead are not dead at all, "but sleeping." (But they, the so-called living, were dead indeed.)

◆

To speak of today: it is no longer Hitler's death train we ride, the train of the living dead. Or is it?

It is. The same train. Only, if possible (it is possible), the train is longer, faster, more commodious. On schedule, every hour on the hour, speedy and cheap and unimaginably lethal. A ghost train still bound, made as March weather, for hell.

The ghost train and the easy riders. The train beats its way across the world, crowded with contented passenger-citizen-Christians.

And then alongside the tracks, a few solitary figures, like stalking scarecrows trudge along. Hunched against the cold, on their own.

The train hoots in derision and thunders by.

◆

We know something of the fate of the train. The train, the one Franz saw, and then refused to board. It did reach a destination of sorts.

He had named the destination aright. The proud cavalcade steamed into hell, on schedule. It delivered its passengers, millions of them, to the appointed place.

They died; they died before they died.

Indeed the destination lay in the decision, the end in the means. They died climbing aboard, died along the way. Died eating, died singing, died drinking, died chatting (about everything except one thing), died beaming and smiling on the children (the children too died). Died of the worm that dies not, died of the serpent's promise (you shall not die).

Died the second death, of which John the Divine speaks.

Alas, alas, had so many ever died before? Died of a communal choice and no choice, of a rollicking freewheeling choice, of a decision and no decision, of routine and misreading of event? Of . . . a shrug?

◆

And then Franz, the obscure refuser. This nonpassenger on the train to oblivion.

Was his No a private whim, inconsequential, a minor change of plans; as though at the last minute, he decided to travel by another route, a later train?

Standing there, in full sight of all, he tore up his ticket, his entitlement. Refused the trip, refused the destination.

◆

His No was a crime. A capital crime.

It is wartime. Everyone must be aboard. Every train is a troop train.

The barque of Peter is a troop ship.

The train is thus, in a manner of speaking, transformed; it is an amphibious vessel, seaworthy, land-worthy. It carried citizen-believers to their destination, a common goal. The voyage, by land and sea, is a matter of the integrity of faith and civilization, the very survival of state and church.

Matters, as the priest told Franz, too weighty for uneducated folk (implied, like him).

◆

In his Bible, he pondered the grammar of Christ — subject, verb: "You shall love your enemies," and so on.

That must mean something! Or why was it said? Must mean something, here and now: Austria, wartime.

If the words mean we can climb aboard the express train of war, and Sieg Heil! with the others, and all this in good spirit (a butchers' train, a slaughterhouse on wheels) — then why did He say that?

◆

More than fifty years have gone by. And the church is still afraid of him.

Afraid of someone so unafraid.

Others of the noble dead are summoned forth from the grave and crowned with sainthood. Not Franz.

Here and there, they are inching toward him....

So hard to approach such a one.

What is the problem, the impediment? Weapons in hand, weapons in heart? The shadow, the monstrous crooked blessing raised (not over Franz, who refused it)? Raised over the generals, then and now?

He stood in his bare bones, unblessed, and said No, and died for it.

While others hurried, stampeded aboard this "Salvation Express," panting and steaming in the dark, snorting like a thoroughbred at the gate.

◆

It is better that he rest awhile, in the shadows. (Though he by no means dwells in shadow.)

In the shadow of a church that cannot summon him, hearken to him, honor him — until we banish the shadows from our soul and, at long last, put subject to verb, and object after; and shout for all the world to hear: "You shall love your enemies!"

On that day Franz will be neither feared nor placed at distance. He will be son and ancestor and brother to all.

Where he stands, where he has always stood: leading the common life commended by the gospel, following the common discipline, walking the common hope.

◆

I would thus imagine him.

Alert of soul, hearing the great despairing wail of that engine, featureless and ghastly as the beast of Apocalypse — that engine named War, battening on darkness, sweeping all into its maw (all but himself, all but a few).

And then his No, that word that turns the soul over.

◆

He knows the limits of that "No": a word small as a grain of sand cast in the triturating wheels of the mammoth engine.

A No surrounded, hedged in, cornered, like a captive under the spears. Not loud, not world-shattering, unheard above the great seductive roar of Heil Hitler! (And yet heard.)

Uttered with no assurance that a thunder clap of consequence will follow, for, against, blood and glory.

It did follow, all of it.

◆

All aboard! On the instant!

The train after all is quick and fast and safe and cheap. It leaves punctually and arrives on the minute. There are ample, even luxurious, first-class accommodations (remarkable, in view of a country at war). The second class is entirely satisfactory. Even the third class, given everything, is acceptable.

And all arrive in the best of spirits! It is just like the start of a holiday — half the fun is getting there!

◆

Then those others — beneath mention really, beneath contempt.

One of them turns, shakes his dummkopf stubbornly, walks away from the splendid hissing symbol of the good life, the genius of the Fatherland!

Where is he bound for, off there in the dark? Not a passenger raises the question. What business of ours?

The silence is eloquent. That one, who dares oppose a great and complex system, an immortal generator of heroes, an empire such as the world has never beheld: *Anathema sit!*

◆

As for ourselves, we know too well, or profess to know, the destination of the train. But is such knowledge to be equated with faith, and the diligent performance of works of faith?

Or equated with — faithlessness?

◆

As for Franz, he will not go away.

He will not go away from the church that sent him on his way, alone. His way, which should have been the way of the church.

So he lingers, half unwelcome. Like a speechless mouth, like a mysterious cry hovering on the air, seeking a hearing.

Listen: "Love your enemies, do good to those who maltreat you. Walk another mile. Refuse the easy ride, damnation as destination."

Is this to be accounted the resurrection of Franz — that the gospel should at long last gain a hearing? A modest event to be sure, apt for our time and ourselves, sorry hangdog, diminished, spoliating as we are?

◆

Franz Jägerstätter

One thinks of "normalcy," and is unashamed.
Behold the riches:
      a loving spouse,
three children, a modest
cut of land —
      and one is no hostage
to fortune ill or fair.

Dignity, stature.
      The church affirms it,
open arms wide as the Crucified,
the rent heart flowing with ointments,
bread, wine — guarantors all,
town criers of salvation:
      Draw near, eat
drink, be healed!
The state, for its part?
      Hands off.
Normally. (And for that takes no hostages.)

      Except when
with a crash
      the "Great Except When"

like a guillotine descends,
    demolishes
the rule of "normalcy,"
       the "hands off."

      (War.
"Uncle Sam Wants You." Or "The Third Reich
Wants You.")

    Is another voice raised,
a differing claim mounted?
       Yes, but generally
no weight accruing
    on the pan marked Prevailing.

    Claim of Christ?
A slight second thought,
    a cobweb of doubt
crossing the forehead, a featherweight.
    Mere breath blows it out of mind.

But not this mind.
      Franz decoded
    (fingers touching a Braille
under blind eyes) the gospel,
    a first casualty
dead as dead Christ on the page,

out of sight, out of mind —
    the "dossier of Jesus Christ"
      closed
        "for the duration."

    Sanctuaries?
    Mortuaries,
      dead
to vocation, to honor, to the high summons
of the angel of annunciation.
Not Franz, not dead.

Die then! let the world know it!

The diminutive naked demon
flees like the undead
this high noon of honor,
the obscene banner
shamed
furled for good.

21

Padre Pio, Mother Pelican

1887–1968

Padre Pio, who died September 23, 1968, and was beatified in 1999, was an Italian Capuchin priest and mystic, world renowned for his holiness, his gift of the stigmata, and a flock of spiritual children almost too numerous to imagine. In this image he holds a medallion of Christ as the Mother Pelican feeding her chicks with precious blood. — WHM

∼

Someone asked the Padre about the conversion of Russia, and received the reply, "Yes, Russia will be converted. . . . However, Russia will teach the United States a lesson in conversion."

Like his patron Francis of Assisi, Padre Pio bore in his hands and feet the wounds of Christ. And more, and worse: for years Pio bore as well the brunt of official church rejection.

A theory spread and gained wide credence: his wounds, which bled profusely during Mass and at other times, were "psychosomatic." They came about because he was obsessed with the passion of Christ.

Seldom at a loss, the Padre retorted: "Go out in the field and look closely at a bull. Concentrate mightily. And see if horns grow on your head!"

To most, his plight was hair-raising. Lavished on him was every traditional aspect of the "showcase saint." In addition to the bizarre open wounds on his body, the Padre had the gift of *scrutatio cordium:* he knew the secrets of those he had not previously met. He also made extraordinary predictions, healed illnesses, held converse with Jesus, Mary, and the saints, even bilocated throughout the world.

Padre Pio, Mother Pelican

Then the era of wonders closed. Some months before his death in 1968, the wounds disappeared as mysteriously as they had opened.

His canonization process goes forward.

And one thinks, no wonder. In 1947 a young Polish priest, Karol Wojtyla, arrived at the monastery to make his confession to Padre Pio. Afterward, the Padre predicted that this priest would one day be pope. He is: Pope John Paul II.

◆

Padre Pio speaks:
"Wounds are a sorry vesture;
look, every move I make
ends in a bloody blur.
Christ makes a clown of me, a public show.
Somewhere between 'crucified' and 'risen,'
knowing much of one, nothing of the other,
neither fish nor fowl (poor fish, poor fool),
they wheel me about like a dressed doll.

"At altar side
I must make and mime Christ's let blood.
I rend the veil of sense; the stalemated
for better or dire, I tell their days to come.
I know sin, too, the stench of it,
the taste, the rot at root of tongue.

"O that the common life were mine,
that I could knock at village doors,
cowled and cinctured, begging bowl in hand,
a friar whose faith
indistinguishable, trod the common way,
muttering in unison his Aves —
faith stopped short
of this eruption and ecstasy!"

22

Holy Martyr Rutilio Grande, S.J., and the Holy Child of El Salvador
1928–1977

The martyrdom of Salvadoran Jesuit Rutilio Grande further catalyzed the ongoing conversion of Archbishop Oscar Romero, who, in many ways, took up the martyred priest's ministry and preferential love for the outcast and the poor. Rutilio is shown here with the innocent, wounded Savior, so symbolic of the suffering country of El Salvador. — WHM

In his early years, he was a type easily recognized by Jesuits: rather conventional, self-absorbed, emotionally dry, duty-bound, distrustful of joy.

Possibly the spiritual regime he adopted in the novitiate (such men are fiercely hard on themselves) only worsened his plunges into depression.

A "mystique of introversion" seems to have been his bent.

One hesitates to call it the true mother lode of the order's "way of proceeding," with regard to prayer and personal discipline. Ignatius had been vague in such matters, counseling moderate penance and fasting and, for the most part, prayer on the run. Let the brothers, in effect, find God in the neighbor and his cries for help.

Still, most Jesuits of Rutilio's (and the author's) time were urged to ascetical harshness. With respect to the world, a kind of siege mentality took hold: go slow, walk uneasy, the times are hardly apt to welcome you or your message.

Once ordained, Rutilio was appointed to the seminary of San Salvador, as "director of social action projects." It was a rather cumbersome

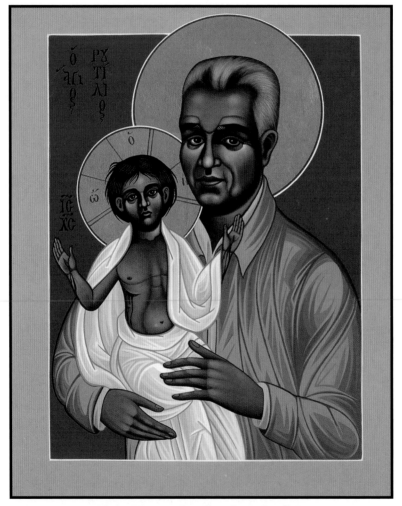

Holy Martyr Rutilio Grande, S.J.,
and the Holy Child of El Salvador

title for a simple task; he was to help point the young men to the poorest and most neglected people, the urban poor, the disenfranchised and unemployed.

His success was spectacular; after nine years, it was generally conceded that Rutilio and his charges were forming a new church in Salvador. Other influences were at work, to be sure. But this kind of priesthood was unprecedented; priests were studying the injustices of the social and economic scene, speaking up, standing resolutely with the landless and exploited.

Unprecedented.

Were the oligarchs, the "first families," to conclude then that the church could no longer be counted on?

Change was a perilous undertaking. It was beyond imagining that political power, economic clout, vast landholdings, would be conscientiously relinquished, because a handful of upstart priests was meddling in matters far beyond their rightful purview!

Disappointment yielded to rancor.

Immemorially the church could be trusted — for silence, for social ornamentation, for the sacraments, for sermons rife with soothing palliatives, for deploying a morality that changed nothing and cost little.

If opposition is a sign that one's work is flourishing, it became clear that Rutilio's ideology was on the mark. He was eased out of the seminary.

By that time certain things were clear to him: what must be done, what part he must play in the future of the Salvadoran church vis-à-vis injustice and violence.

A marked change in himself. No more diffidence, introspection, scrupulosity; no one owned him, not even those dogging second thoughts of unworth or sinfulness. Take it or leave — he was his own man.

He was appointed pastor of an impoverished town, Aguilares, not far distant from his birthplace. There he was in his element, pastor, shepherd, counselor, a man who chose sides.

Dangerous indeed; the contradictions were heating up; one might even venture that Rutilio was stoking the fires.

Aguilares, for all its dust and mud and hunger and landless peasants working for pittances, also was the domain of an elite. Great misery, great wealth, the inhuman imbalance of things, from time immemorial in place.

And then this priest, this interfering spoiler, his catechists, his base communities, their harping on redress, on "this need not be, must not be!"

Enough, more than enough. A resolution was in order; it was brutal, final.

On March 12, 1977, Rutilio and two of his flock, an old man and a boy, were gunned down on the road to El Paisnal.

Let priests of a certain ilk and inclination, let even a bishop named Romero, take note.

◆

This is what the priest dared say, in church,
in the awful year 1977:
"I'm quite aware that very soon
the gospel won't be allowed to cross our borders.
We'll get only the bindings, because
all the pages are subversive.
And I think that if Jesus himself
crossed the border at Chaletanango,
they wouldn't let him in.
They would accuse the Man-God
of being a rabble-rouser, a foreign Jew
who confused the people with exotic ideas,
ideas against democracy — that is,
against the wealthy minority, the clan of Cains!
Brothers,
without any doubt,
they would crucify Him again.
And God forbid
that I be one of the crucifiers!"

In a sublime leap of imagery,
Rutilio holds in arms the divine Child.
So far as is known, no such vision was granted him.

But
look close, Rutilio insists:
this is no "ordinary" Child; not even,
if one can so speak, an ordinary divine Child.
This Child bears the wounds of an Adult,
in hands and side — no "ordinary" wounds, to be sure.
Wounds of the Crucified One!
Wounds of the Risen One!

Now the point becomes clear, the irony:
Rutilio, dead in his blood,
holding the Child (his wounds surely lethal) —

and the Child lives. His arms are stretched
cruciform and — no cross!
Robed all in flowing white, a martyr's mantle,
enthroned in the arms of a martyr!

The Child, surrogate and symbol
of martyred Salvador.
"Now" (say the eyes of Jesus,
the burning eyes of Rutilio),
"is the point clear?"

23

Maura "Soshin" O'Halloran
1955–1982

At the age of twenty-four, Maura O'Halloran, an Irish-American woman, raised and educated as a Catholic, sought admission to a traditional Buddhist monastery in Tokyo and embarked on the rigorous training of a monk. With extraordinary speed she achieved a breakthrough to enlightenment, astonishing her aged Zen master. Her published journals, Pure Heart, Enlightened Mind, *describe her training and her eventual decision to leave the monastery, after two years, to serve others in the way of compassion. Shortly after, she was killed in a bus accident in Thailand at the age of twenty-seven.*

— WHM

In the world of Zen, language is apt to go topsy-turvy. For years now, we have followed or been followed by (or both) a group of Buddhist monks and nuns. They benignly shadow us as we set out, endlessly it seems, to rid the world of its plague of nuclear weapons. A lifelong task, a work that calls for a sturdy heartbeat!

Sturdy our friends are; they strike their drums with intense vigor. On Broadway they sound like the heartbeat of all the living, prevailing against odds of clamor and turmoil.

In the courtroom in Portland, Maine, where the Prince of Peace Plowshares were on trial in 1997, the drumbeat outside pounded relentlessly. In the ears of many in the court, the drumming took an ironic turn. It was contradictory, a rebuke; it was as though the drummer were shaking her head, beating a stubborn truthful No against the machinations of judge and prosecutor.

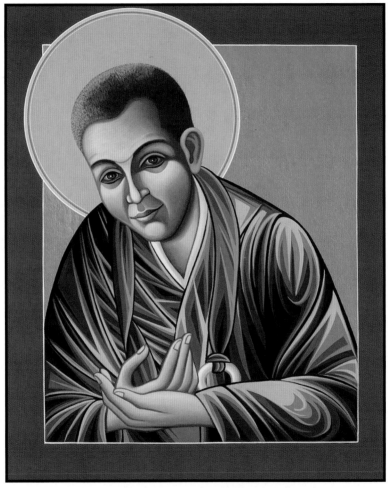

Maura "Soshin" O'Halloran

How blessed we have been for some twenty years now, with the friendship of these Zen friends. Their drumming and walking and fasting and vigiling are a splendid insistent urging: Do not give up. Walk the world for peace. Manifest, dramatize the beat of the heart of things — orchestrate life over death!

Boston to Dublin to Latin America to Tokyo to Thailand: so went the voyage of Maura O'Halloran, a matter of miles, a matter of soul. She was Irish-American. The Irish part of her was a restless world-voyager, in the image of the old monks since Patrick and his kind — a constant setting out to an ever new stage of understanding.

She underwent strict Zen training in a Japanese monastery, when such a venture on the part of a woman was rare, if not unique. The discipline included harsh manual labor, meditation, lengthy pilgrimages, begging along the way. She took such things in stride.

And what saving humor! Here she is, at work in the zendo kitchen:

Dinner — even I must admit — was delicious and beautiful. . . .
Roshi, from the other end of the table, beaming, said in English, "Zank you vely much." He's radiant. "You're welcome," I muttered in Japanese, and all oohed. It was a success. Jiko and I hugged, shook hands, laughed, and after cleaning, sat down with flowers and finished the sake. Bejaysus it was grand.

And she can be telegrammatic, and offer an apothegm: "The notion of a nation is to a country what ego is to a body."

She takes to the road; in Korea she comes on friends everywhere, who welcome her into their homes and spoil her with kindness. In one house, "Jimmy came home from work, and we had a warm evening, sitting, chatting, drinking Campari. Reclining in luxury on the black leather sofa, we talked about austerity — a delightful way to do it."

Sage beyond her years:

Someone said that we must take care of things simply because they exist. This occurred to me as I was sweeping the floor. In the dust pile there were 16 grains of rice and two tiny crawling things that didn't need to die. It felt neither good nor bad.

I look at the clock. It is two o'clock. A long time later I look at the clock and it is only two o'clock. It is always two o'clock. I feel a great peace.

Maura reminded some of St. Thérèse of Lisieux, that other young woman who consummated a lifetime of ardor in a few years. The passion of each was to offer some measure of relief to a suffering world.

Maura reminds me also of Thomas Merton, Christian and Zen monk. He wrote me in the following vein, three years before his death:

I feel as though I've already died. Someday someone will come in and discover me at the desk, stone dead, will touch me and I'll fall over.

And Maura:

I'm twenty-six and I feel as though I've lived my life. Strange sensation, almost as if I'm close to death. . . . So in a sense, I feel I've died. For myself there is nothing else to strive after, nothing more to make my life worthwhile or to justify it. At twenty-six a living corpse.

◆

So we have a venturesome bridge
flung across cultures and worlds.
It is as though Maura trudges along an arc,
or a rainbow stretched across skies, Ireland to Japan,
and she taking on
         (her soul taking on)
hues and hints of a vast spectrum —
Irish Catholicism touched, tinctured,
         brightened to a halo,
   with Zen zest and single-mindedness.

Great riches, concentrate of soul, in small scope
of time and place.
Vivacity, mindfulness,
the half-smile of one who parlays, takes chances

within
    at no loss, none
of presence to the world.

     She leans forward
as though from window or portal, the unadorned
gold of eternity behind.

     Two hands
cupped, half-supplicating, empty
        invite
Come. Be.

24

Ĥoly Martyr Jerzy Popiełuszko
1947–1984

"*Father Jerzy Popieluszko, a popular young parish priest in a suburb of Warsaw, Poland, spoke out against the abuses of communism and supported the then-banned Solidarity labor union. Thousands flocked to hear his Sunday sermons. He was abducted by the Polish secret police on October 19, 1984. His savagely beaten body was found eleven days later in an icy reservoir. Father Popieluszko's death serves as testimony to the struggle for freedom, basic rights, and human dignity*" (used with permission of J S. Pauluch Co.).

Father Popieluszko is shown clutching a rosary, which seemed to be his own natural form of sustaining prayer during the years he was harassed and threatened for his standing "in Solidarity." Pope John Paul II also sent him a rosary as a sign of his support and affection.

This icon of Holy Martyr Jerzy Popieluszko was created with the hope and prayer that Father Jerzy will be a patron and intercessor for all diocesan priests throughout the world, especially those who suffer and stand with the outcast and persecuted. —WHM

∾

The young priest, a look of sadness,
inwardness,
        substance, soul.

His garb Polish-traditional,
cassock, stole, rosary in hand,
        accouterments
long out of mind,
the image redolent of silence's
deep well.

Holy Martyr Jerzy Popieluszko

A moment,
and his voice breaks in a tidal wave,
rock-ribbed conviction, passion.
"To serve God is to seek a way
to human hearts."
        And large-handedly, his
seeks your hand.

Malevolence
festers, a bomb aimed, explodes;
        but
        "Fear only betrayal
for a few silver pieces of meaningless peace."

Not an inch given,
        no bending to the will
of martinets, overlords, all-out liars
defaming, cowing a people.

The end.

        Volcanic days and nights;
a brutal, inept, bloody misadventure;
                murder.
        This troublemaking priest
once for all, done with.

Fools, every one.
        Never, not to be done with,
no blow sufficing, no mortal strike
        but crowns him, immortal,

        Jerzy, people's martyr.
        Alleluia.

25

William Stringfellow, Keeper of the Word

1928–1985

On the back cover of A Keeper of the Word: Selected Writings of William Stringfellow, *we are told, "The theological legacy of William Stringfellow — Harlem street lawyer, social activist, and commentator — is enjoying a revival among a new generation of Christians." This image represents Bill Stringfellow as keeper of the Word, symbolized as Holy Scripture burning and glowing inside of him, open to the words of Deuteronomy, which he contemplated and lived.*

This fiery prophet to America continues to admonish and console through his living presence in the communion of saints and in his writing, which is searingly surgical and thus . . . healing.

— WHM

William Stringfellow was a theologian annealed in the fires stoked against truth-tellers.

His style fairly asked for trouble.

In method and inclination he was unorthodox and undocumented, laconic, a man of unsettling convictions freely dispensed.

Not surprisingly, he went unrecognized and untenured in the academy, whose practitioners tolerated his mordant exegesis only on occasion.

Now and again invited to university or seminary, his arrival was awaited with pangs of trepidation among many, his departure marked by a communal breath of relief.

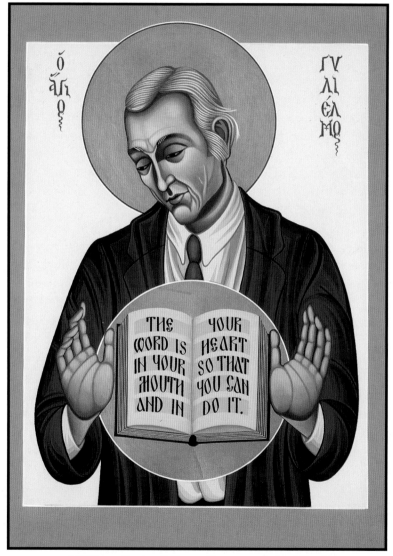

William Stringfellow, Keeper of the Word

His work is the subject of no seminary courses, to my knowledge; in the mainline theological libraries his books are conspicuously absent.

Yet he kept writing with thoroughness and passion. And for years he traveled the country, speaking out on a multitude of generally unpopular subjects.

He and Anthony Towne, his companion, were early advocates and friends (and the sole biographers) of a notorious enfant terrible, Bishop James A. Pike.

Early on, Stringfellow supported the ordination of women and gays. At every turn he encouraged new initiatives on behalf of the poor and dispossessed. He corresponded affectionately with the likes of Dorothy Day and remained through thick and thin (mostly thin to be sure) a faithful friend of the Berrigans.

He was a great listener, and a passionate cook as well. At his table, whether in New York or on Block Island, might be found any of the above specimens, various drinking cronies (in the early years), now and again a coven of clerics, writers, island workmen, and political organizers, friends all.

Immediately after his graduation from Harvard Law School, String-fellow moved into a Harlem cold-water flat and began lawyering on behalf of the poor.

In that unlikely circumstance a theme emerged. It would govern his theology and become his prime contribution to biblical understanding. He came on Paul's discussion of the "principalities and powers," a virtually neglected theme. Stringfellow reflected on the clutch of institutions, their control over the hapless and poor — the welfare bureaucracy, landlords, schools and courts and jails; and onward and upward, to the awesome dictatorships of death rows, the Supreme Court, CIA, the Pentagon, Wall Street, the quadrennial charade of "democratic elections."

Each "principality" controlling and controlled by the others, nicely dovetailed in aim and ego, institutions governed by lies and fueled by violence, claiming literal life-and-death power in the world. Institutions that illustrate and dramatize before our eyes, the status and condition of humans: we the Fallen.

Through a lifetime he explored that genetic intuition, his translation of the mind and heart of Paul. Death rode the saddle of the horsemen

of Apocalypse. American institutions were effecting a vast larceny of
the earth's resources, of human talents gone awry, all to the spawning
of metaphors and methods of death.

The Vietnam War, the rotting inner cities, the expendable poor,
racism and sexism and homophobia, these were more than the cul-
tural evidence of the Decline and Fall of America. They were spiritual
realities, the "other side" of glitter and show and empty rhetoric and
religious euphoria. Biblically these were revealed as evidence of death
in our midst, claiming us for its acolytes — claiming at least our com-
plicit silence, our dull incomprehension. Evidence irrefutable of our
"Americanization."

After years of debilitating illness, Stringfellow died in 1985 on Block
Island.

I summon his memory with a pang. For courageous intelligence, his
like will not soon be granted us again.

◆

Death and Life of a Friend

My last death was Stringfellow's.
    Death, rattling his begging bowl.
    "Sustenance, sympathy!" he whined.
    Stringfellow bethought: death
        lacking a name
    (unnameable, nameless horror,
        they mutter in terror)

    he named it finally, taming
        the appetite that feeds
on kings and clowns
    feeds and feeds, never satiated —
    women, warriors
    the sleepy-eyed unborn —
    never enough!

    "We must break this thrall
once for all" became his mind's
    holy obsession and vocation.

Like a priest's crucifix aloft
    before the obscene undead —
Christ expiring for love, summoning a last
commanding cry — "Down, dog death!" —

       thus Stringfellow —
years and years, crucifix in hand
    miraculous he moved in the world
    dismaying, dispelling death.

Thus as a sun advances, shadows
       go underground.
He stands, believe, in resplendent noon.
      Taken from the cross
he ascends straight up.

And death, shadowy, starved, named,
    is not,
       and no where to be seen.

26

Holy New Martyr Nestor Savchuk

1960–1993

Nestor Savchuk was born in the province of Crimea, southern Russia, in 1960. As a youth he excelled in boxing, wrestling, the martial arts, and painting.

In his twenties he began to work as an apprentice painting religious murals in Odessa. There the older artists told him the stories of the Russian saints. Inspired by the saints with a love for God, Nestor set out for the thirteenth-century monastery of Pochaev to become a monk. This love grew naturally and expressed itself through his devotion and prayer with the holy icons, which one day would be the source of his martyrdom.

After his ordination his spiritual father advised him to go to the isolated village of Zharky. There he found a church which had many ancient icons and which filled him with a mystical feeling or invitation. There he also found many obstacles and difficulties. The church caught fire once and became the target of an icon-stealing ring connected to the Russian mafia.

Nestor would stay up at night to guard the church. He was touched with a desire to ask for the grace of martyrdom. He began to pray for long hours. A friend warned him about this prayer and told him he should not ask to suffer. Nestor replied, "Yes, I understand that, but maybe if I will pray for martyrdom — perhaps I will be able to pray it out." On December 31, 1993, Nestor was found murdered outside his house in Zharky. — WHM

Holy New Martyr Nestor Savchuk

Nestor Savchuk

I dare hold aloft the holy icons
unbearable, the weight of a world,
the weight of — becoming.

　　Become! That which you hold

— turn, turn about —
holds you aloft, this holy sleight of hand!

I veiled my hand and arm, I thought to honor,
to cherish, to obey the holy ones
　　　　amid infestation
of dishonorable men, for filthy lucre
larcenous, in darkness absconding,
the blessed images defiled.

They murdered me.
　　　　From the earth
my blood cries out, the blood of innocent Abel.
The cry:
　　Would that it inundated, a healing unguent
dissolving all defilement!

27

Companions of Jesus

Triptych for Boston College Community

This triptych includes the glorious North American Jesuit martyrs Jean de Brebeuf (1593–1649) and Isaac Jogues (1607–1646); Richard Eisenmann (1936–1972), compassionate worker with the poor of Brazil who was killed in a car accident; Padre Miguel Pro (1891–1927), the mischievous and delightful martyr of Mexico; and Amando López (1936–1989), professor of theology and martyr of El Salvador.

— WHM

❧

At center, arms extended, Blessed Miguel Pro, thirty-six, Mexican. Executed by firing squad November 23, 1927.

A year previous, President Calles had issued the infamous "Thirty-three Articles," aimed at destroying the Catholic Church. Religious education was abolished; orders such as the Jesuits were dissolved; public worship was put under the heel of the state. The church in effect was driven underground.

In no wise daunted, Miguel set about inventing ways and means of continuing his priestly work. He improvised disguises and went about with the sangfroid of a born clown.

Once, invited to address cab and bus drivers, he arrived dressed as a mechanic. Afterward he wrote gleefully: "There were 150 of them, the type that affect Texas hats, long hair and spitting through their teeth. . . . I saw to my amazement that I hadn't lost the old flow of coarse resounding words. . . . Blessings on all the bus drivers of the world!"

He had a deep compassion for the poor, begged on their behalf and wrote of their plight with acerbic irony: "They have the bad habit of eating three times a day, generally with good appetites. . . . They wear shoes that wear out and clothing decorated with holes. . . . They get sick and need medicine. . . . So I impose on doctors and on rich people who lend me houses."

That same year, the resisting Catholics pulled a quite wonderful stunt. Over Mexico City some six hundred balloons were set loose, each with a packet of religious pamphlets attached.

Official egos were tweaked: pandemonium, outrage!

It was a backhanded compliment to our elusive bandito-priest that he was immediately suspected and apprehended. The moment was electric with danger. He was released, reluctantly, one thinks; but hailed back twice, as the prank boiled away in the skulls of the humorless apparatchiks. Miguel wrote a friend, "It was a farce. . . . During it I pulled our worthy rulers' legs, humorously telling the truth and compromising no one."

But the game was over. He was arrested and summarily condemned.

As he faced the guns he held a rosary aloft. His last words were "Viva Christo Rey."

For the underground church, the words became a rallying cry, echoed by thousands at his funeral.

◆

At far right, holding a chalice, St. Isaac Jogues. He endured one of the longest travails on record: four years of virtual martyrdom, 1642–1646.

He sailed from Dieppe for the Huron "new world" mission in April of 1636. After a voyage of eleven weeks, he finally arrived in Quebec. A perilous canoe trip awaited; with five Hurons he set out for the Tobacco Indian country.

As Charles Garnier knew, Isaac must learn that he was plowing a field of boulders. Lalemant remarked dryly, "These missionaries are the abomination of those whose salvation they seek — and this at peril of their own lives."

In June of 1642, Jogues, together with a group of forty Indians, was ambushed and captured by Iroquois. The long travail was underway; the captives were led from village to village, trophies of a vicious bush war, to be exhibited, mocked, and tortured. The miles were an endless gauntlet of torment. Jogues's left thumb was chewed off; he was

Companions of Jesus

Companions of Jesus

grateful to be spared the right one, so he "could still write to the brethren."

For a year, Jogues was reduced to a slave, and a useless one at that, wounded and drained.

Then in August, thanks to a compassionate Dutchman, he made his escape.

These Dutch Protestants — one thinks of them as genuine Christians indeed. With their help Jogues embarked down the lordly Hudson toward New Amsterdam. From thence he set sail for his beloved France.

He appeared at the Jesuit community at Rennes, this scarecrow revenant, "a Lazarus raised from the dead." One of the brethren reported, "He is as cheerful as though nothing amiss had befallen him." And more vatically, "He certainly expects to cross the ocean once again."

Correct. Jogues happily sailed off again in spring of 1644. Two quiet years followed, ministering to the young colony of Montreal. Then in September of 1646, he was urged to undertake a peace mission among the Iroquois. Premonition dogged him: "My heart tells me that if I am to be sent, I shall go, but I shall not return."

"A terrible beauty was born." With a crude, strangely befitting irony, details of the end were received piecemeal, some time after the brutal fact. Somewhere in the wild, Jogues and de la Lande had been tomahawked and beaten to death.

For Jogues, the cup was brimming and the wine good. One lifetime, two deaths.

◆

At far left, holding aloft a cross of aspen wood, St. Jean de Brebeuf, the elder among the saints.

He was robust of frame, a peasant inured to hardship. And a heart valiant beyond telling with its steady beat of purpose. Of that heart, much will be written; it has passed into legend.

His story is simple and straightforward, like himself. Thirty-three years of age, he left France.

He was to be in and out among his beloved Hurons, a hostage of fortune. One is dismayed to see how the missionaries are at mercy of secular weal or woe. If the French prevailed, they could move freely about the land; only let the English gain the upper hand, and the Jesuits are stuck in place.

A good year — 1634; a treaty had been signed and the French were in control. Time to set to work.

Brebeuf and two other Jesuits embarked from Three Rivers, bound for Huronia, eight hundred arduous miles. There were rapids, waterfalls, endless portages. All in a day's work; they trudged in water and mud, slept on mother earth, hefted their belongings downstream "thirty-five times," dragged the canoes "at least fifty times."

Brebeuf: "To be sure, I was at times so weary my body could do no more. But at the same time my soul was filled with great happiness.... No one can know this feeling unless he has experienced it."

Parched years were to follow. Then in 1637 a near miracle: the first adult convert. A decade later, the neophytes numbered in the thousands.

Violent swings of fortune were inevitable, one thinks. Foreigners, palefaces, were at mercy of any misadventure befalling the native peoples. Let there occur a crop failure or a defeat in battle, the missioners stood there, targets of chagrin, easy prey.

And always, there were the Iroquois to take into account: crafty, spoliating, blistering warriors. In March 1649, some twelve hundred of these descended on the village of St. Ignace. Brebeuf and Lalemant were dragged off, together with a number of Huron cohorts.

Torture is hardly to be thought a modern invention. The martyrdoms that followed make hard reading, even in our brutal century. The captives wore garlands of hot hatchets, were mutilated and scalped; baptism was mimed with boiling water.

Finally they tore out the heart of Brebeuf, and ate it.

The fierce tribute cannot be missed, then or now: Who knows but that this heart, numinous and robust, will create heroes, even of such as ourselves?

◆

Six Jesuits perished before dawn on November 16, 1989, at the Central American University in San Salvador.

Of one among them, Amando López, something intriguing was said: he was the one "who knew best how to live."

As for the others, several were in an immemorial Jesuit mode, plodding along, bound to the wheel of the world — workaholics. Amando's story is a familiar one to anyone acquainted with the decades of crisis that swept Central America in the 70s and 80s.

In Nicaragua and El Salvador the church was rent in two; an old guard stood firm among the bishops, the oligarchs, even the Jesuits. Such were determined to hold fast to the way the church had "always" functioned, the way of perks and privilege and no questions asked — especially questions raised in the gospel itself. . . .

Thus Amando, no guardian of a church-cum-palace, was all but tossed overboard as the SS Salvation made its way through troubled waters. A sequence of events, pro Amando and con, ensued: almost, one thought, as a law of nature. He was appointed rector of the seminary in San Salvador, then removed from same. (And one cannot but think: here is an all but endemic trait of the best Jesuits — to shake the powers on their high perches, and so end in trouble.)

On to Managua, and rector of the Jesuit high school there. Then a boost: rector of the university. And trouble again, and he plucked thence.

A cooling-off period followed, a sabbatical in Spain. Then back to Salvador, and a chair of theology.

Probably the last years were the happiest; surely, at least to those who knew him, these were the most fruitful. He discovered the rural poor, served them on weekends with Mass and baptisms and marriages and funerals.

He preached from the heart; it was evident that he remained unquelled, grateful to have beached in calm waters.

Calm, to a degree only; a year before his death, he told a reporter:

We believe in some of the goals of the FMLN [the revolutionaries], but I cannot fight and I cannot tell others to take up arms. But that does not mean that we do not understand the position of those who do. . . . We sometimes talk of leaving, also. But our hope is not in leaving, it is here. If I leave, the crisis will stay. Here I may be able to effect change.

The artist is exact: Amando is pictured not as administrator or teacher. In a colorful stole rather, as a man of sacraments; more, one who himself became a sacrament.

He kneels, he looks at you, hands extended. The entire gesture asks, What do you need of me? Forgiveness, the Eucharist, the waters of baptism? — or perhaps my death?

He was his own man. And as far as may be known, he was ready when, once for all, the bullets raced in, called a halt.

◆

Kneeling to the left, a North American Jesuit of our own time, and the youngest member of the triptych.

Does he belong here? He enters the icon as it were by a back door. (As the vast majority of us will, by dint and favor of Christ, who for sake of saints, scoundrels, gyrovagues, and the lost, keeps the portal wide open.)

Well, it was by request of his brethren that this young Jesuit, Father Richard Eisenmann, kneels here among the great ones.

He holds aloft the sigillum of the Jesuit order, the Greek letters for the name "Jesus," surmounted by a cross and an aureole of light. He has little else to offer than this; he stands by The Name. No certified saint, no martyr of the strict sense.

Yet he was much beloved by the poor of Brazil, whom by report he served with all his heart. Padre Laurenco they called him affectionately. He chose to live as one of them, in a shack shoved to the rear of an alley, in a slum in Bahia, of the notorious northeast Brazil.

He died young. Not much of a story, a thirty-six-year-old priest, an accidental death in a far country. None of the glamour, gore, glory of the others, those to right and left of him in the painting, who died so hard and rose so high.

◆

Through these
    we are granted a second chance;
        through these
God takes us at our word, seriously.

"Company of Jesus" — then
        you mean the words, the
        terrible entitlement, harsh accompaniment?

        Through these we venture
past simulacra and vain posturing
        into — meaning.

        We bear
                for only credential
                        their testament
        signed, sealed —
                at long last
                        delivered?